Theatre for Community, Conflict & Dialogue

Theatre for Community, Conflict & Dialogue

The Hope Is Vital Training Manual

MICHAEL ROHD

HEINEMANN
Portsmouth, NH

HEINEMANN

361 Hanover Street
Portsmouth, NH 03801–3912

Offices and agents throughout the world

© 1998 by Michael Rohd

The idea is to get this work out there. Have no hesitation in using the
process, the activities, and the work described herein. However, to
create new manuals or curriculum utilizing this specific writing in any
way, shape, or form, please contact the author at 10801 Linson Road,
Owings Mills, MD 21117.

Library of Congress Cataloging-in-Publication Data
Rohd, Michael.
    Theatre for community, conflict, and dialogue : the Hope is Vital
training manual / Michael Rohd.
        p.   cm.
    Includes bibliographical references.
    ISBN 0-325-00002-6
    1. Psychodrama. 2. Group psychotherapy for teenagers.
3. Participatory theater. 4. Theater and youth. 5. Drama in
education. 6. Hope is Vital (Organization) I. Hope is Vital
(Organization)   II. Title.   III. Title: Hope is Vital training
manual.
RJ505.P89R64   1998
616.89′1523′0835—dc21   98-6132
                                                          CIP

EDITOR: *Lisa A. Barnett*
PRODUCTION: *Vicki Kasabian*
BOOK DESIGN: *Jenny Jensen Greenleaf*
COVER DESIGN: *Darci Mehall*
AUTHOR PHOTOGRAPH: *Carolyn Bell*
MANUFACTURING: *Courtney Ordway*

Printed in the United States of America on acid-free paper

10   VP   13

To the memory of
Bryan Fant

Contents

Foreword

In the 1960s a heretical notion began to spread about the theatre—first about theatre in the U. S., and then about "theatre." By 1966 the notion evolved into a widely circulated question, and Simon and Garfunkel asked the question point-blank in their insurgent *Sounds of Silence* album: "Is the theatre really dead?"

The seeming ironies of the question are, in retrospect, multiple. A few examples: Does a 2,500-year-old art form "die"? Could such a form, in the mid 1960s generating the most explosive decade and a half of experimentation in western theatre history, be gravebound? Could Broadway, with some of the best-loved productions ever, and a flourishing regional system be considered moribund? Numbers of theatre majors in colleges were soaring and professional M.F.A. acting degrees were multiplying like mayflies. Could anyone seriously ask, "Is the theatre really dead?" Absurd!

Indeed, there were absurdist plays from Europe about the theatre, along with God, actually being dead. Inspired by the catastrophe of the second World War and its subsequent existentialism, this Theatre of the Absurd demonstrated even pointless life could be vividly theatricalized. But something was afoot. The "official" theatre of Broadway and regional repertory rang false for some. Perhaps it was theatre's decline in the face of television. Perhaps it was the lack of relevant theatre practice at the grass roots. Perhaps it was the very pointlessness to which the absurdists referred.

Whatever the cause, some practitioners such as John O'Neal of the Free Southern Theatre and Luis Valdez of El Teatro Campesino abandoned the official spaces and the standard models and began to organize theatre for their local communities, people connected by common oppressions, common struggles, and common goals.

In the U. S., a small new path had been created. As with Nietzsche's "light of the stars," however, it would require time for us to realize the implications. Mao Zedong in China had written thirty years earlier that fundamental changes in cultural and artistic expression would not occur in terms of *what* was presented, but *for whom?* and *by whom?* Bertolt Brecht had been wrestling with this same question when he designed plays and performances for workers, social activists, and the oppressed. He more than anyone in Europe was responsible for not only blazing the first major new trail in official twentieth-century theatre, but also for paving the road with academically embraced language: *alienation, epic theatre, gestus, lehrstuck,* and so forth. But official theatre practice remained the interstate in U. S. theatre. While pathfinding, Brecht's work tended more often than not to find paths on the same terrain—performances by trained actors, by the professionals, for the watchers. O'Neal and Valdez, the S. F. Mime Troupe, and in the 1970s, the women's and gay/lesbian theatres were incorporating less-trained and even untrained performers in their work, and taking that work to new communities who had never before seen a theatre that was *for* and *by* them. The community was in the audience and on the stage, and the theatre was in the community. The theatre wasn't dead. Its roots were just going deeper and deeper.

Just a decade before, in the 1950s and in a country far, far away, Augusto Boal was evolving a theatre practice that would take an even more radical step. It was called the Theatre of the Oppressed. Not only did he educate people how to take up the power to make theatre, but he created forms whereby the audience—now spect-actors—could stop the production, enter the action, propose new points of view, enact alternative solutions, and discuss the possibilities with those still in the audience. While we can't credit Boal with inventing a highly improvisational approach to theatre, we can credit him with formulating an extensive political aesthetic for theatre and with inventing forms of theatre practice, such as Forum and Image Theatre, designed especially to include people who had

never been in or even to a play and who, by reason of their oppression, cried out for dialogue.

Michael Rohd is steeped in that dialogical tradition.

His theatre education at Northwestern had been relatively traditional, but he was influenced by the practices of Viola Spolin,
interactive theatres such as Second City, and by a personal need
to create theatre that honestly mattered to people. Inclusive approaches to theatre seem to have been in the air. By the 1980s,
various methods of pedagogy, social work, and psychotherapies
had so incorporated forms of role playing that the practice was
becoming truly mainstream. Responding to the need for HIV education, Michael began Hope Is Vital, and by the mid 1990s the
workshops were fully interactive, designed for the nonactor, and in
several ways running parallel to the Boal tradition. In 1995 during
the Pedagogy of the Oppressed Conference at the University of
Nebraska at Omaha, Michael Rohd met Augusto Boal, saw the
Theatre of the Oppressed techniques in practice, and commingled
the two approaches. The result is what you are about to read and,
hopefully, use.

One of the basic assumptions of Michael's approach is that
virtually anyone can participate in this kind of theatre. Theatre
education, theatre experience, even theatre familiarity are not required. What is required is a desire to engage in dialogue about the
oppressions in our lives and to use theatre as a tool to effect that
engagement. However, this is not to say the techniques are some-
how not demanding. To the contrary, even the introductory games
can be very demanding, but only insofar as the participant wants
to make them so. Cover the Space—one of the interactive origi-
nals—is such a basic and brilliant game that after ten years of using
it, I am still astonished by the ease with which it raises fundamental
questions and the enthusiasm it generates. (Take note: Cover the
Space is just a warm-up in Michael's book; the hot stuff lies further
on.) As a result, the difficulties are not in the theatre. The difficulties—and essential difficulties—are in the oppressions the group,
class, or community wants to confront, and in the struggle to
reestablish dialogue.

Speaking of dialogue, a second basic assumption of Michael
Rohd's theatre: the intrinsic need of the human psyche—body,

mind, heart, spirit—for dialogue. In the most existential way, Michael argues that we make each other through dialogue. Without human dialogue, we would not be human; rather, if we could stay alive, we would be that with which we had had dialogue—animals, trees, air currents. I am fond of telling the story of the wolf boy. According to legend and some history, a baby was lost by an explorer team in the nineteenth century and was considered to have perished. But several years later, explorers came upon a pack of wolves, and amidst them was a human boy who was otherwise a wolf. The pack had adopted the baby as one of its own. In behavior, communication language, identification—all were from the world of the wolf, not the world of the human. Whether or not the story is factual, the essence remains: While nonhuman animals adjust to their surroundings, they do not become other animals. Humans, on the other hand, create themselves by means of the dialogue made possible by languages, art, and culture. Or by wolves. Our dialogue is what we become.

If dialogue is essential, then its absence is a violation of the most profound sort. We must be able to signal back, to speak out, especially in situations where we feel we have been wronged. It is so essential that, when dialogue stops and is replaced by the oppression of monologue, we can feel deprived of our very humanity, which, according to Michael Rohd, is in fact what happens. In turn, those conditions, organizations, or individuals who engage in monologue will likely not reestablish dialogue or relieve the oppression.

The task, then, is for the oppressed—whoever feels the object of a monologue—to confront our oppressor and to get on with the ironic task of reestablishing dialogue with the oppressive force.

Michael began his work by applying interactive theatre to issues of sex education and HIV—thus the transformation from HIV the disease to HIV the Hope Is Vital process. Few monologues have been as unrelenting as the fifteen-year AIDS epidemic, nor perhaps have so many new monologues issued from a public-health wreckage: demonization of gays and lesbians, stigmatization of HIV-infected people and people with AIDS, refusal of government leaders to even speak the word *AIDS* for four heartbreaking years, cultural fear of sexuality, young people resorting cynically to unprotected sexual activity, rise of the right-wing morality of blame, accusation, and shame. Michael Rohd rose to the occasion. He took his considerable skills as an educated person of the theatre and began to apply theories of interactivity. In time he had cultivated an entire practice in which people, and especially the young and vulnerable, could use the tools of the theatre to create dialogue with friends, peers, and even strangers on the forbidden subject of AIDS. Peer education exploded within the workshops; participants found they had much to teach and to learn from each other. Along with countless other relentlessly creative, committed, compassionate minds (most working in relative anonymity), Michael had found yet another weapon in the war on this cruel disease.

He went on the road, worked across the United States, clarified his methods, invented new ones, borrowed useful ones, researched HIV and behaviors related to its discussion, expanded his repertoire to include many public health issues, made contacts that he maintains to this day, and created, finally, what could be called the arsenal comprising Hope Is Vital.

Most important for us, however, is that he found a way to put all of this into a workbook. A teaching and learning book. A workbook that works.

Understand, I don't believe I have seen even a theatre book on, for example, acting or directing, that is as functional as what we have here. I have taught countless acting classes and given many workshops. I have even taken a workshop from Michael, and I was here in Omaha as he worked on this amazing compilation. I knew the difficulty would be to put the process of a workshop into the kinds of words that allowed someone essentially unfamiliar with Hope Is Vital—or unfamiliar with Augusto Boal or acting or theatre—to "get it." I must admit to having been a bit skeptical. But when I read his initial draft, I knew he was breaking the code. Putting myself in the position of someone who had never seen these practices, I read through descriptions that were so clear, so detailed and yet so readable that, yes, the nonpractitioner could follow this path. And, yes, this path could inspire experienced and inexperienced alike to exciting, revelatory work.

But no, we cannot learn these wonderful techniques through osmosis. We must be willing to read the processes carefully and then at some point to jump into the practice. If an interactive workshop, and especially one of Michael's, is in the area, take it to enhance your understanding. But be willing and eager to get better, to learn more, and to know the importance and limitations of being a useful workshop leader. Read especially carefully the side notes included throughout the book. These are, to my mind, some of the most important elements Michael has devised. Implement what you find to the best of your ability. Afterward, reflect. While you, we, all of us, must "jump in" to learn this work in practice, it is also necessary to "jump out," to sit down with the book after a workshop and review the processes described, absorb again the amazing side notes, and evolve your critical perspective on what you do.

What you will find, I believe, is that you are on the right track. That you "get it." That Michael's pathbreaking contribution is theoretically solid and practically not only effective but empowering.

You will also perhaps find that the theatre is not at all dead. That it lives in us and around us every moment of our lives. That to find it is to get on its path and, as Paulo Freire says, "We make the path by walking." And finally, that to learn the language of theatre as articulated by a master teacher, is to learn human dialogue in one of its most powerful and joyful forms—the theatre of everyday life.

—Doug Paterson

Preface

History

In the winter of 1992, I was teaching theatre at the Sidwell Friends School in Washington, DC. A close friend of mine, also a teacher at Sidwell, was running periodic art workshops at a downtown clinic for men and women living with HIV who also were living on the streets. The clinic is called Health Care for the Homeless, and it's located on the fifth floor of the 14th Street Union Shelter. She suggested that I volunteer and offer some drama workshops for the clients.

I went down and met April Martin, the social worker at the clinic responsible for client (patient) activities. We started right away: a couple of men, one woman, me, and April playing games. The group grew and after some time we moved into storytelling. As it became clear we were moving forward with something (although none of us knew what), the clients began to ask me if I could bring some of my teens down from school. At the same time, a group of students I worked with regularly at Sidwell were challenging an idea that I mentioned often in my classes: the notion that "theatre is healing"—a phrase they claimed I utilized every other day and one they said left them thoroughly confused. Seeing an opportunity, I offered them a chance to join me at the clinic, not as healers, but as participants to share the experience. After navigating school and parental hurdles, sixteen teens, give or take a few depending on the day, came down.

We played together, we laughed, we told stories, we shared awkward silences, we improvised, and we began to create theatre about the way all of our lives intersected with HIV and AIDS. We played characters in stories that drew from group truths and we fictionalized ideas that came from discussions. By the end of the spring, there was a comfort level in the semiregular group of participants, and a sense of exploration, of dialogue. As the school year drew to a close, one of the clients at the clinic suggested that in the fall we take our work out into the city schools as a sort of prevention workshop. My initial response was "No." I don't believe in "message plays," and I thought his idea would rob our work of its complexity and uniqueness. He explained that our work would stay the same; we would take theatre dialogue workshops out to youth and give them a chance to participate—to explore decisions, issues, and life situations. We could sharpen our focus and use our energy to engage others. So that's what we did.

With an ensemble of twelve teens, three men from the clinic, April (and her three-year-old son, Aaron), and me, we worked together twice a week, two or three hours a shot, for six weeks starting with the new school year. Then, confident in our ensemble's teamwork and ability to dynamically create safe and active spaces for dialogue, we took our performance workshops to public high schools and junior high schools, correctional facilities, youth shelters, and even some groups of adults. We worked with groups ranging in number from ten to fifty, often turning down requests to present at assemblies or fairs. Our response was simple in those instances: The work is interactive, the numbers at such gatherings are simply too big, and the setting must be conducive to full participation from all present. By the end of that school year we had conducted approximately twenty performance-workshops around the city.

The group continued its work after that without me. I decided to help other communities set up similar programs. I left my job and Washington, DC, and drove across the country to drum up enthusiasm and opportunities for this work. I landed in the Northwest and began to work in schools and other settings, training groups of youth and preparing adults to use these techniques. As the work grew and my experience in communities expanded, the power of this form of theatre to address a multitude of community concerns became apparent. I was asked to develop programs focusing on violence, substance use, teen pregnancy, and other issues around the country. Urban and rural, East Coast and West Coast—people are, of course, as unique as their communities. Thus, the beauty of this work as a medium for dialogue is that it is specific to the individuals with whom it occurs and to the moment in which it occurs. The tools are transferable and their use ends up where it belongs—in the hands of community members who pose the questions and create the forums needed in their own communities. That's where Hope Is Vital currently focuses its attention: spreading the program and the techniques to interested individuals and groups. That's the reason behind this manual.

Note: "Prevention" refers to what is commonly thought of as a community's educational attempts to deal with youth and social concerns by addressing (and stopping) them before they occur. There are a variety of approaches to prevention work. This program is one.

Goals

In this book, when I refer to Hope Is Vital, I mean the program as an existing organizational entity and the techniques that comprise the work.

Hope Is Vital is based on the belief that education is dialogue. Paulo Freire, educational theorist and author of the groundbreaking *Pedagogy of the Oppressed,* spent a lifetime shouting to the educators of the world that we learn by doing, not by being told or even being shown. This basic belief holds true for all subjects—particularly what we have come to know as "prevention education." Information is not enough. It is useless without the power to act. Hope Is Vital seeks to provide opportunities for people:

- to create safe spaces;
- to have dialogue;
- to explore choices and the consequences they can bring;
- to practice for real life;

- to enhance their skills of communication and decision making;
- to understand how self-esteem affects moments of decision;
- to take risks in fictional worlds with the potential to learn rather than fail;
- to take action and to be the protagonist in one's own life;
- to critically and viscerally analyze life situations and one's own responses;
- to utilize the multiple perspectives different individuals bring to every interaction as a positive tool for problem solving.

Mission Statement

Hope Is Vital poses questions.
It does *not* offer answers.
Audience/Participants propose answers.
Together, everyone looks at options.

It does not declare right and wrong.
It does not seek single solutions.
It seeks discussion, trust, and
a step forward in each person's ability
to take care of themselves and
to look at their world with compassion.

Theatrically,
the goal is to work together to create theatre,
which will engage, strike, and stimulate
the audience;
to give them the desire and the need
to participate actively—
in their work,
in these moments of theatre,
and in their own lives.

Philosophy

To borrow from Robert Alexander, founder and director of Washington, DC's Living Stage, "Every human being is an artist and in the moment of creation, we are at our most sane, most healthy, and most fulfilled. When we share a piece of our vision of the world with others, we are better able to see ourselves, to interact with others, and to make our own choices."

The act of expression is an act of connection—through it we become positive, active participants in our lives and in our communities.

To borrow from Augusto Boal, creator and practitioner of the system of theatre known as Theatre of the Oppressed, "Theatre is a language through which human beings can engage in active dialogue on what is important to them. It allows individuals to create a safe space that they may inhabit in groups and use to explore the interactions which make up their lives. It is a lab for problem solving, for seeking options, and for practicing solutions."

Theatre allows us to converse with our souls—to passionately pursue and discover ways of living with ourselves and others. We are all artists, and theatre is a language. We have no better way to work together, to learn about each other, to heal, and to grow.

Acknowledgments

My thanks start with crediting sources of inspiration for the spirit, and in some cases, the ideas and activities that help make up this work.

In particular, Augusto Boal, teacher and friend, to whose work I came (through his books and workshops) after starting Hope Is Vital, and in which I found affirmation, clarification, ideas, and impetus to move forward and grow.

Also, Robert Alexander and Living Stage, Viola Spolin, Dwight Conquergood, Cornerstone Theatre, Dorothy Heathcote, Paulo Freire, ED (the seminal Chicago improv group), and Ann Woodworth.

Thanks also to the organizations and people who have supported Hope Is Vital, especially in its early stages, with trust and opportunities: The Sidwell Friends School, Washington, DC; Rick Honn, Bob Williams, Sally Selby, John Elko, Health Care for the Homeless, Washington, DC; Lookingglass Theatre Company, Chicago, IL; Arts Expand, Los Angeles, CA; The Fant Family, Marion County Health Department, Salem, OR; Kristen Nelson, Janet Bubl, 4J Schools, Eugene, OR; Nancy Johnson, Lane Educational Service District, Eugene, OR; Kathryn Henderson, Marty Johnson, Oregon School for the Deaf, Salem, OR; Planned Parenthood of Columbia/Willamette, Portland, OR; Georgetown University, Washington, DC; Carol Day, Patrick Kilcarr, Pamela Wilde, Jon Aaron, Douglas

County Health Department, Omaha, NE; Laurie Foral, Children's National Medical Center, Washington, DC; Coos Bay, OR; Haverford College, Philadelphia, PA.

And thanks to the individuals who have supported me throughout this work: Tom and Samantha Kane, Andy White, Avis Turner, Elizabeth Allbrecht, Cherie Ulmer, Irene Addlestone, Ann Cusack, Reverend Chris von Lobedan, Doug Paterson, Kathy Randels, Joel Sugerman, Juliea McCall, Tristan Lemons, Bill Rauch, Allison Carey, Ben Cobb, Chris Moore, Anne Titus, Paul Edwards, Bruce Manclark and Cory Eberhart, all my friends, and my family.

Thanks also go to those who made the original manual possible: Mary Lou Boynton for the computer it was typed on; Andy White and Kerry Catlin for their time and thoughts; Connie Lehman for her excellent design; and Tracy Wiseman without whom it wouldn't have happened.

And thanks to the original Hope Is Vital ensemble who began the program in 1992. The original program continues in collaboration with peer educators from Burgess Clinic at Children's National Medical Center in Washington, DC, now known as Teens Against the Spread of AIDS (TASA): Molly Whitehead, Shonna Carter, Meena Nankani, Sona Nankani, Lauren Arrington, Veronica Alvarez, Leila Rached, Rachel Kravetz, Kerri Archer, Emily Hawkins, Daphne Lockyer, David Sabel, David Kupperberg, Shennan Weiss, Russell Golatt, Tim Willaford, Jerry, April Martin, and Aaron.

Introduction

The purpose of this book is to give educators, community workers, artists, youths, and others interested in community dialogue and problem solving a clear look at the process and specifics involved in Hope Is Vital interactive theatre techniques. The activities come from a variety of sources: some from the arsenal of Theatre of the Oppressed, some from Living Stage, some from Viola Spolin, some from other curricula, and some are original. This book offers a way to look at these activities to help you create a practical, usable format for your own work.

Mostly I have been asked to use these techniques in community projects that fall loosely under the following three categories:

1. Youth Ensemble Training: An intensive training of a youth ensemble (eight to twenty middle school, high school, or college-aged youths), who will use interactive theatre as a resource to conduct performance workshops in their school or community around specific issues. A community adult is trained to continue working with them in a leader/facilitator capacity.
2. Adult Training: Training adults from the community to use this work with youths in school, social service, and other community settings.
3. Workshops: The facilitation of one-time workshops for

youths and/or adults around community issues and conflict, which may take place in schools, organizational settings, or in open community forums.

The activities and techniques in this book form a structure that you can alter to suit your needs whether you work in forty-minute classroom blocks, train a group to lead ninety-minute workshops, or have a weekly two-hour meeting with an ever-changing group of youth. The structure is an arc, which can apply for individual sessions as well as for a longer project, and looks like this:

Warm-ups → Bridge Activities → Activating Material

This book explains how to use the pieces of this arc as a progression as well as demonstrates how the arc can serve you in a variety of situations. The book is sequential and parallels the process you might go through with a group. *Reading it from beginning to end first will help you determine how to best shape your goals and expectations.* The blueprint for creating your own workable plan includes these two key elements:

- knowing your goals and the time frame you have (both in each session and in the long run)
- recognizing that these activities are not random games to pull out and play just for fun, but rather building blocks that you can place into your group process to further your work along. It is a progression. Only with forethought can you create the environment and develop the skills where the work has its deepest impact, where it can "go deep."

The majority of this book defines the categories of this arc, gives examples of activities that fit into each category, and discusses how they contribute to the forward motion of your individualized plans. The process you establish should seek to break down the boundary that normally exists between actor and audience to create a workshop of participants. It should move toward the activating, improvisational scene work (Activating Material) that demands active participation. These are not role plays, where participants follow a predictable script, with a "solution" that's been dictated by someone else. These are pieces of theatre that come from questions *you* ask about topics your group cares about; the goal is to look closely at choices, strategies, and communication. To get to that place, you first must build trust, focus, and skills. The process is a journey. Like any journey, it has a beginning, a route, and a schedule, but it does not have a predetermined destination. It just gives a direction to start. This book is meant as a general map, which will change with every journey you take.

As I've said, I use this work often with middle school–aged kids and those older. Aside from working early on to build concentration with middle schoolers, I haven't needed to greatly change these techniques with different age groups. Educators of elementary school–aged youths have told me that with minor adjustments, taking into account age-appropriateness of issues and developmental differences, they've had great success bringing this work into their classrooms. Those adjustments and judgments are yours to find and create.

This work is also powerful with special needs populations. The emphasis on caring and self-expression throughout the group process allows individuals to safely be heard in unique and supported ways.

Warm-ups

The purpose of warm-ups is threefold: to get a group of people playing together in a safe space, to energize that space, and to create a sense of comfort in the collective doing of specific and structured activities. The goal is to demechanize the body and mind and to engage responses that are fresh and utterly in the moment. These activities have nothing to do with "issues." In fact, one could argue they aren't even "theatre." They simply aim to get people out of their seats and interacting in a different way and to prepare them to participate as the work gets deeper, more focused, and more "theatrical." It's all about creating moments where participation is impossible to resist, moving forward into the process you have set up, and having fun along the way.

I use the word *you* to refer to the individual teaching and leading the activity. The leader can be the adult running a group of youth. Or a leader may just teach each activity once and then have group participants lead after that. "You" can also mean a youth who leads activities with others. When I say "they," I mean the participants. "You" is the leader, "they" are the players.

Physical Space

You don't need a theatre to do this work. It's not about performing but, rather, playing. All of the activities require an open space; the actual size is completely dependent on the number of participants. A simple rule is that you need enough room for playing to have the necessary boundaries and for goals to be achieved—goals that are challenging, but possible. The space shouldn't be cramped but it shouldn't be some vast empty area. Usually a large classroom with all desks and chairs pushed to the side will work with a group of 10 to 25 youths. For a group larger than that, you'll need a bigger space. You'll have a better sense of how space positively affects these activities as you begin using them. Be aware of that dynamic and always set yourself up to succeed.

> Focus *is defined here as one's ability to concentrate on and stay involved in the task at hand.*

A Safe Start

When beginning this type of group work, it's important to take some time and discuss what participants want and need to see happen in order for the space to feel safe. In other words, do they feel that there should be guidelines for the way they treat each other? If you've already been working with the group, you may have already had this discussion or feel that this idea of respect for others is already in place. Think carefully. Has the discussion taken place, or did you at some point begin your relationship with these participants by telling them what *you* expect? This is a nice opportunity to put the idea of dialogue on the table, both in theory and in practice. I usually facilitate this conversation during the first session, after the first couple of activities. The group is warm but not yet in deep. If you are training a group of peer educators who will take this work outside, these rules are even more important. They should form a core set of group goals for the peer educators to bring to each

> *Safe Space: A working environment where participants feel comfortable playing and honestly sharing their thoughts and feelings.*

session they lead. In the section on peer education, I outline some ground rules I think are important.

Game Descriptions

My descriptions are based on my own experience of what has worked and hasn't worked for me. They are suggestions, not rules (especially for number of people and ages), and should be ignored if you want to try something different. This work is about what will succeed for you. This blueprint is, again, a starting point.

Sources

As I stated in the introduction, many activities in this book come for the work of others. Theatre games and exercises are passed down from teacher to player, and through the work of new practitioners, they change and grow. Almost all of the activities here are different to some degree from the versions I first learned. I list at the top of each activity my main source or influence for that activity. If the source is listed as "unknown," it is a common game whose origins are lost, at least to me. Those activities listed as "original" are techniques I can comfortably say I developed from scratch, but even these have been influenced and inspired by others I've already acknowledged. (The sections on Activating Material and Facilitation, for example, bear similarities to Augusto Boal's Forum Theatre. There are, however, marked differences.)

This sourcing is important for two reasons: it gives credit where credit is due; and it provides a history, tracing where specific ideas came from and where they might go. Ideally sourcing can help you follow the work back, if you are so inclined, to search for connections, and it may help you better move forward in your own new direction. We all learn as we go and in so doing, give thanks by giving back.

Thoughts About Games in General

These warm-up games play an important part in the process of using the techniques. The games listed are simple and effective ones to start sessions with and return to with groups over longer periods of time. Like anything you introduce to a group, there is a fine line between playing them again and overplaying them; you will be able to tell when a game has worn out its welcome.

There are many more games out there that fit into this category. Some you may know as icebreakers; as long as they involve physical play and have clearly defined tasks and a need for focus, grab them. Use them. You will also find plenty of activities that can fit into this category in some of the resource books listed in Appendix C.

When you begin working with these activities, you may sometimes find groups confused and reluctant to engage in "playing games" when they thought they were coming to deal with "issues" or something else serious and quite different. Or, they simply may not "get" why they're being asked to do "dumb kid stuff." I recommend that you always take the time to discuss (or at least explain) the process at the beginning. Talk about the reason you're playing games and how you are hoping it will lead to a level of participation and activation around the work you will all be doing together. This is especially important if this work represents a significant structural departure from the way you normally work with this particular group. Respect them enough to realize you don't have to keep goals of interaction from them; rather, that discussion can lead to an excellent dialogue around education or at least about what can make group work safe and fun.

I also stop after games and ask for comments or observations; I'm real big on processing and taking moments to share discoveries that may have occurred for different people at different points. This often just becomes a moment of silence in which people think a little but don't actually verbalize. That's valuable as well. The trick is to not allow these discussions to dissipate the energy and forward motion of the activities and the session itself. You have to be aware of the group's needs and decide where you want to go in each moment as it arises. This is of particular importance if you are training a group of youth (as peer educators) to do this work throughout your community. They should be constantly examining the process at every step so they are prepared to pull it apart and put it back together again as leaders.

The Word *Process*

The word *process* has two separate, but similar meanings in the context of this text; first as a noun, *process* describes the structure of this program and this work; the way pieces of the progression relate to each other; the journey that is the work, as opposed to a fixed product. As a verb, to *process* describes the dialogical interaction that occurs in an individual or within the group as events and responses are experienced, critiqued, reflected on, felt, and shared.

The processing of the process = moments of learning.

The Reminders are things to say in your group while they are involved in activities. You may want to establish their function early on by saying something to the effect of "I will often be giving you directions during games. Listen and adapt, but don't drop out."

Energy and Focus Work

This first group of games works on energy and focus. They offer a method to establish the concentration that you will need with your group to move deeper into the process. Every game is an opportunity to work on focus and discipline in a nonpersonal, nonrules sort of way.

I'll explain: A good game sets up a clear task with clear boundaries and moves everyone forward together with objectives and ways of achieving them. Therefore, when someone is not in the game (and he/she is giggling, disrupting, chattering, casually playing) they are not focused. You have a responsibility to remind them to stay in the game and that you're playing together. If you're playing, you are in it. If you're not playing, you're not in it, and you're preventing others from playing as well. You can use the structure of the game to demand full participation. Therefore, you're not insisting on following a rule because "it's appropriate" or "you're picking on one youth" but demanding full participation because that is simply how you play the game. You can also make it clear to your group that the level of concentration you expect, even now during these "silly, fun, little games," is necessary for the group to be ready for more intense concentration later when you go on to the more complex exercises. Task-related discipline can be very effective throughout this process if you commit to it from the beginning. Talk about it with your group and always stay aware of your ultimate goal of setting up a safe space; a space where everyone can enjoy themselves as they work and prepare to have an active, honest dialogue around things about which they care. Remember—this work is about the spirit of play within a set of rules.

Circle Dash

Number of People: 10 or more (an ideal group: 20–40)
Age Level: Great for all ages
Time: 5–15 minutes
Source: Unknown (Taught to me in Coos Bay, OR)

The Basic Idea

Everyone stands in a circle around one person who's standing in the middle. The object of the game is for any two people in the circle to silently signal each other and switch places. The person in the middle tries to get to an open spot before the switchers. The person left takes the spot in the middle. This is a silent game.

Reminders

- You can teach the game from the middle spot and demonstrate as you explain.

When you call out "freeze" during any activity, you're asking for your group to stop and maintain position—to be still, but to stay engaged, not to drop out of the activity. Go over this definition early in the process so that it's clear to everyone.

- You can play this game with your group after you teach it.
- Those switching places have to try to get to the spot they are aiming for. If the person in the middle gets there first, they can't go for a random, empty spot—they must take their turn in the middle. That keeps a sense of order in a fast and chaotic game.
- A player can't just run—they must make visual contact with someone and signal a sort of agreement. This demands some connection between players.
- More than one pair can go at a time. With large groups, the fun comes when lots of pairs switch at once.
- People should go *around* one another, not *through* or *over* each other. (This may seem obvious, but wait for the first collision!)
- A good way to end the game is to say "See how many times you can switch in the last thirty seconds."

Thoughts

This game is contagious and succeeds on many levels. The most important aspect is that it allows people to choose their own level of participation. They can choose to switch places often or they can choose to not signal anyone. The key point here is that by just being in the circle, they are participants. Because they are making a choice one way or the other, they are involved. It's rare to see someone not switch by the end of the game.

If someone gets "stuck" in the middle you have the ability, as the facilitator, to help by trying an especially hard switch you know you won't make. If you feel it necessary, this gives you a way without "cheating" to prevent someone from getting too uncomfortable. Stay away from refereeing. I never referee, but stay silent and let them work out disputes. This also engenders participation, because when participants realize that there is no "official" call and other players are waiting for one, the participants must make their own decisions.

Cover the Space

Number of People: 10 or more (an ideal group: 20–50)
Age Level: 12 years old and up (This game can work with younger people, but often focus becomes an issue.)
Time: 5–15 minutes
Source: Boal

The Basic Idea

You set up a big rectangle in the room, using four chairs or trash cans as corner markers. You have everyone start walking around in the designated space. The rules are no talking, no contact, and to keep moving. After a little while you tell everyone to be aware of their own body, the bodies around them, and the space on the floor. Then, you ask them to begin to make certain that the space on the floor is covered. They need to keep moving at all times, get to corners and sidelines, and to always move to empty spaces to "cover the space." If you were to shout "Freeze!," they should be evenly distributed around the space, filling it. You shout "freeze," point out how they're doing, and send them right back to covering the space. It's a game of freezing, getting new instructions, and finding their rhythm again.

Variations

Variation 1: After a little while, you shout "freeze" and tell them to grab a partner's hand. As pairs, they keep covering the space. Repeat as triads. You can move to groups as large as you want, spending some time on each one. To end, they drop hands and cover the space solo again.

Variation 2: After a little while, you shout "freeze" and ask them how fast they can create three triangles using all their bodies without talking about it. You say "go."

After they do it, return to cover the space solo for a little while. Then, freeze and form three squares, and so forth. Other options could include forming different shapes, combinations of shapes, letters, words, numbers. To end, return to cover the space solo.

Variation 3: After a little while, you shout "freeze" and ask them to quickly put themselves into groups based on what they're wearing on the top half of their body without talking about it. You go around to each group and on a count of three they all have to say out loud what they think their group is called. For instance, "long-sleeved T-shirts" or "red tops." Then, if the group is new to each other, have them quickly learn each other's names in their group. If they know each other, return to cover the space. This round goes on with footwear, hair, favorite kind of music (silently), favorite kind of movie, and so forth. I always end with eye color.

> *Take your time. Remember that the rules are for the goals, not for obedience.*

Reminders

- Lead this game from the outside since there are a lot of instructions and freezes. You need to be able to watch and sense when to go to the next step.
- The size of the rectangle is dependent on the size of your group. It can't be too cramped. They must have room to struggle to cover all the space. But it can't be too big either, or the task becomes impossible.
- The game should remain silent at all times.
- The game should take energy—it should be tiring as well as energizing. All of this play is work and should be played at 100 percent. If they don't feel that they're giving out that much energy, they're not playing.
- In the beginning, remind them to look at each other. They may not be able to talk, but they should notice who they're in the room with. Ask them to relax as well as to look at the other participants.
- Each time they come back to cover the space remind them to find their rhythm and focus.
- You will sense if people are playing and trying to cover the space or if they're just walking around. This game offers a great opportunity to remind them not to play casually but to play the game and get their bodies involved, to move and focus on the task at hand.

Thoughts

I start every first session with this game, all the way through the three variations. Whether it's a long training or a one-shot workshop, this game gets people up and involved in the least threatening and ultimately most sneaky way possible. It simply asks participants to walk around the space and move individually; together as a group, yet safe in their own space. Over time it adds a group task, physical contact, working together, and groups connecting and finding each other. You can play the whole sequence once or you can play the first part and use that rhythm to return to a focus point in subsequent sessions to add other variations. You can ask participants to lead the game down the line and come up with new specifics in each variation. This game also allows participants to shake off the day and begin to find a rhythm in the group movement. They can be in this space and relax out of whatever tension they might bring.

One evening I was asked to observe a university-based, peer ed group I had trained conduct a performance workshop with thirty-five freshmen on their campus. They had chosen this game to use as a warm-up. The space they were in was a small dorm (or residence hall) lounge. As they began the game, it became clear that not only was everyone able to cover the space with ease, they were jammed in like sardines. As the participants grew restless, bored, and frustrated, the student leader grew impatient with what she saw as their unwillingness to get into the "spirit of play." She pushed them to focus and demanded that they work at the game. It was like asking a group of people to play football with no ball, no end zones, and no teams, and then being furious that they weren't enjoying themselves. The freshmen grew more and more antagonistic and a negative tone was established that lasted the whole session. Set yourself up for success. Recognize what environment you need to provide for that spirit of play to be accessible. Be aware of where your group is and try to not get defensive if something isn't going as planned. Adapt.

Tilt

Number of People: 10 or more (an ideal group: 14–40)
Age Level: All ages
Time: 10–20 minutes
Source: Unknown

The Basic Idea

Two lines of the same number of people face each other on opposite sides of the room. Each line numbers off from 1 on up. The numbering off should begin at opposite ends of the two lines. In the middle of the space rests a bottle or a cup. You explain to participants that they are standing on the edge of a plate and that the bottle is the center point of the plate. The object of the game is to keep the plate from tilting out of balance and crashing off its fulcrum. You call #1 from one of the lines and when he/she steps onto the imagined plate, the #1 from the other line has to step out and move to balance the plate. The person who is called first is the leader of the pair. Each pair has to keep a straight line between themselves and the bottle in the center point at all times. Then you call the other numbers until everyone is playing at once. The leaders are all from the same line until you call out to switch leaders. You can switch leaders often and have participants play with varying speeds and different ways of moving. This is a silent game.

This is the first of many activities where pairs all play at the same time. This reduces self-consciousness and ensures that everyone gets lots of time to do, not just to watch. It particularly pays off when you move on to bridge activities and improvisation.

Reminders

- You should lead this game from the outside if possible but you can lead it while playing.
- They should try to remain in visual contact with their partner at all times.
- They should try to challenge but never trick their partner.
- See if they can switch leaders fluidly without stopping or jerking about.

- If you don't see them varying their speeds, ask them to move in slow or fast motion or on the ground.

Thoughts

This game gains energy with more people. It gets people moving and connecting. It's play with safety, because everyone is doing it at once. As a leader, it might feel like it would get boring quickly. Let it go a little longer than you think it should. Watch their focus and joy.

Defender

Number of People: 8 or more (an ideal group: 20–60)
Age Level: All ages (Watch for focus issues for those under the age of 12.)
Time: 5–15 minutes
Source: Unknown

The Basic Idea
Everyone starts walking around the space without talking and with no contact. After a few minutes you ask each person to silently pick an individual in the room whom they will consider their own personal defender. They continue to move around while doing so. Then, ask everyone to silently pick an enemy. Everyone keeps moving around while you let the mystery of why they've done this sit there for a few minutes. Then you tell them that their goal is to keep their defender between themselves and their enemy at all times. First, they play this for a couple of minutes; then you ask them to put different levels of importance on the circumstance. Maybe their enemy annoys them, they owe their enemy money, their enemy is an ex-friend or ex-romantic partner, their enemy is trying to kill them, and so on. Push them to get their whole body involved, and make it important to them. This is a silent game.

Reminders
- You should lead this game from the outside so you can determine when to change the circumstance.
- The game is quick with lots of energy. Remind everyone to stay involved and to be careful when they run.
- Point out the difference they should find in the way their body and energy responds to each new circumstance.

Thoughts
This game introduces imagination work without making a big deal out of it. It's fun, and there's not a lot to think about. You give individuals a chance (whether they know it or not) to find out how easily they can engage their own "pretend muscle" and connect it to action and feeling. You can point all of this out, or you can just observe to know for yourself where the group stands in this regard.

Blind Handshakes

Number of People: 8 or more (dependent on how much space you have)
Age Level: 13 and up (As an eyes-closed game, you must decide if younger ages have the focus and trust to play.)
Time: 5–15 minutes
Source: Unknown

The Basic Idea

Everyone finds a partner and finds some space in the room. They face their partner and make certain there is some room behind them so that if either of them was to walk backward, they wouldn't immediately bump into something or someone. They shake hands and freeze in that position while looking at their partner. They close their eyes. Remind them, as with ALL eyes-closed games, that no one will mess with them. They will be told the rules and will be in control of their participation. On "go," they will release the handshake, keep their arm and hand frozen in the handshake position and begin, slowly and carefully, to walk backward. You will say "freeze." Then you will say "find your partner" and they try to return to the original spot and position with their partner. When everyone has gotten somewhere tell them to open their eyes, check their results, and switch partners to do it again. Repeat this three to five times. This is a silent game.

> A Note About Partners:
> *Participants should make an effort to find partners they don't know well, especially early on, for two reasons: 1) to meet new people, and 2) to more easily focus and not become distracted with people you're familiar with. If your group knows each other, ask them to not work with their best buddies in the room. They should be willing to know people in fresh, new ways and be open to making discoveries.*

Reminders

- You should lead this game from the outside. You are ultimately responsible for making sure no one walks out an open window.
- They should keep their eyes closed at all times. You may have someone who simply can't (or won't) do this. The way to

approach this is not to single them out but keep making the general announcement that eyes should be closed. If they don't, realize they probably can't. If they're disruptive, that's another story. Then, you can discreetly let them know they're preventing others from focusing on the game and that you won't tolerate it.

- They should go slow and careful, knowing they will bump. If they get stuck and cannot move backward further, they should adjust and move in another direction. If they do so, they should try to keep track of their twists and turns.
- I teach this game by getting them all the way to the handshake with their eyes closed then explaining the rest of the game. This way the game starts when you give the actual objective, and you can take advantage of the momentum of the newness of the game.

Thoughts

This is a safe, get-to-know-you, sensory game. I usually do this early in the first session with a group, often right after Cover the Space because it continues to energize the space. It also adds the element of experiencing the space and the group in a new way, which gives a sense that they have gone through something unique together. It's fairly quick and gives the participants the opportunity to start to meet, briefly, one on one.

Minefield

Number of People: 10 or more (an ideal group: 15–40)
Age Level: All ages
Time: 10–30 minutes
Source: Unknown (Taught at a physical education conference)

The Basic Idea

Everyone stands in a circle and tosses any objects they can find that aren't breakable or sharp (shirts, jackets, books, keys, knapsacks, etc.) into the center. Spread the objects out so the whole center space is evenly covered. Find a volunteer and have them close their eyes. The rest of the group, using their voices, tries to navigate this volunteer to a point directly across the circle from where they currently stand. If the volunteer touches any of the objects during the navigation, KABOOM, instant obliteration! You, the leader, play angel of death and watch for fatal contact. The trick is all participants are trying to lead the volunteer at once. They cannot speak to each other or designate one speaker. They cannot call the volunteer or each other by name. They must fight through the chaos and lead the blind volunteer together.

Variations

Variation 1: The volunteer is vocally led by one navigator. Everyone else in the circle holds an object in their hand and gets a chance to throw it into the path of the blind traveler. They can't hit them with it, and it can't be placed right under the descending foot of the traveler. If they do so, their object doesn't count. They must be patient and strategize.

Variation 2: Several blind travelers, each with a volunteer leader. The travelers don't know who their leader is when they start. They have to figure it out. All travelers are led across at the same time while other participants in the circle attempt to toss objects in their path.

Reminders

- No one in the circle can move around, especially when trying to toss objects.
- Everyone involved should work on making the risk to the traveler as important as they can. The task should be done with immense focus and energy, not silliness.
- Make certain *no names* are used during the process. This forces participants to use their voices more fully.

Thoughts

This game is contagiously fun. Once you get going everyone wants to be the traveler, and it usually becomes a matter of stopping and assuring the group that you will play again. If you stop playing just as interest has peaked it's a nice way to ensure energy the next time because people will be excited to play again. You can also put a strong focus on the imaginary circumstance and really use it to introduce the idea of creating pretend situations with "high stakes," a phrase we return to again and again.

Zip Zap Zop

Number of People: 8–30
Age Level: 12 and up
Time: 5–15 minutes
Source: Unknown

The Basic Idea
Everyone stands in a circle. You have everyone repeat the words "zip, zap, zop" three to four times, all together. You demonstrate the game by starting it. You have a bolt of energy in your hands. To start, you send the bolt out of your hands with a strong forward motion straight at someone else in the circle (using your hands, body, and voice) saying "zip." You must have eye contact with them when you pass it to them. They receive it with their whole body and pass it immediately on to someone else saying "zap." That person passes it on with a "zop." The game continues "zip, zap, zop."

Reminders
- You always must have eye contact with the person you pass the bolt of energy to.
- This game is not to be played casually. Stress the importance of playing and being in it with lots of energy using both the body and voice.
- Stay focused. There should be no pauses. The goal is not for them to go as fast as they can but they shouldn't relax, either. The bolt of energy should never hit the ground.
- As in a scene, if someone messes up, they shouldn't stop. It is helpful to articulate this idea now, so that it will be familiar to the group when they get to scene work. They shouldn't get pulled out of focus but rather should go on with the game and regain the rhythm.
- At first people will get the words mixed up or lose concentration. It can be frustrating at first but they must stay on task and not give up.

Thoughts

This is a great warm-up to quickly get group concentration. It's a good ensemble game with long-term payoffs. It's not necessarily as great a game if you're working with a group on a one-shot basis because it takes a couple rounds for the group to get the hang of it. Then it becomes really fun as well as functions as a strong skill-builder. As you work with a group over time and come back to this game with some degree of consistency, you will see a group rhythm develop. You will be able to see when the group is in sync and when they're not. This is a great game to play after a break. It reenergizes everyone almost immediately.

This is a game I've played with casts of shows I've been in and one that I always teach casts of shows I'm directing. It brings everyone together in the space and in the moment beautifully. There was a seminal improvisational company in Chicago in the early '90s called ED, which would often play before rehearsals and performances. I once watched them play for almost ten minutes during a chaotic sound and light check without dropping the energy once, without even pausing. I keep that as a private goal.

Donkey

Number of People: 10–40 (an ideal group: 15–20)
Age Level: All ages
Time: 10–25 minutes
Source: Unknown (Taught to me by Dexter Bullard in a rehearsal)

The Basic Idea

Everyone stands in a circle. You're in the middle. You point at someone, call out one of the figures (see below) and count "1, 2, 3." The person you point at and the people on either side get into the position of that figure. You pick another person in the circle and call out another figure. If any of the three people involved does not get into position before the count of 3, they're out. The game ends with two winners. The game sounds like "elephant, one, two, three"; "horse, one, two, three"; "angel, one, two, three" and so on. Before you start playing you teach the figures you're going to use in the game, then dive in.

Reminders

* Make up more figures. The possibilities are endless. You should start the first time with 5 or 6 figures, and as a group gets better, add more to increase the difficulty.
* Don't try to explain the game, teach it by doing it. Start by having the participants make the figures and test each figure by going around quickly, pointing as if you're already playing.
* Leading the game takes a lot of focus. You want to keep a rhythm, not laugh, and get faster when it's time to make the game harder. The energy you have in the middle is what will keep folks interested after they are out.
* You have to call folks out. It's not an honesty test. The only chance players have when they mess up is that you may be too flustered to notice; so if you miss it, they stay in. This keeps you concentrating and creates a fun tension between you and the participants.
* Never change a call and don't slow down when you say "you're out."

Thoughts

This game is the only competitive game I like. I normally feel all activities should bring players together completely but this game is so much fun and so contagious, I use it often. It's fast-paced, generally silly but focused, and has people using their bodies and concentrating. If taught quickly and clearly, most groups of any age don't want to stop. The key is to note how the people who get out first respond. If they slink away or generally lose interest you need to push the game faster to its end before you lose them completely. If they're enjoying watching the rest of the round, the game is doing what it should.

FIGURE	MIDDLE PERSON	SIDE PEOPLE
Elephant	Arms in front with hands clasped together to form a trunk	Arms in a big "C" position to form ears on either side
Horse	Both fists in front of nose to form a muzzle	Arm bent at 90° with elbow on the middle person's shoulder and forearm straight up to form an ear
Bunny	Both hands behind their back to form a tail	Arm straight up to form an ear
Angel	Both hands together as in prayer, sing an angelic "Ahhh" on 3	Both arms extended straight out at the side to form a wing, sing an angelic "Ahhh" on 3
Gump	Pluck imaginary chocolates from a box while saying "Life is like a box of chocolates."	Run in place
Donkey	No movement at all	No movement at all

Machine

Number of People: 5 and more
Age Level: All ages
Time: 5–20 minutes
Source: Spolin

The Basic Idea

Everyone stands in a circle. One person volunteers to start the machine in the middle of the circle. They begin a clear motion and rhythm that can be repeated for some length of time. The motion and the rhythm stay the same. Once the rhythm has been established, one by one the other people in the circle add to the machine by creating a new movement that connects spatially, *but not physically,* to the existing movements. The rhythm of the first movement is the guide. The game is silent. The idea is to get everyone (or up to ten people at a time) into the machine and focused on staying with each other. After a little while, as a complete machine, the first person can change the rhythm and the group tries to find the new pace, together. Then, you call "freeze," (pause) "relax." Everyone comes back to the circle and starts a new machine.

Variations

Variation 1: Have folks come in with a sound, in addition to the movements, so an orchestra is almost created.

Variation 2: Pick an imaginary type of machine (like a pet-caring machine, or a house-building machine) and have the group create it.

Variation 3: Have the group break into smaller groups and have them all create the same imaginary type of machine, share them, and note the differences.

Reminders
- The game will feel strange and participants will feel self-conscious at first, so you want to do away with audience and

get as many folks out there as possible. I recommend being
the person to start the first machine yourself as you explain it.
- People should try to use the space three-dimensionally and not
just build a straight line off of the first person.
- Encourage people to not create movement with just their
hands and arms but with their whole bodies.

Thoughts

This game is actually a sequence that starts here as a warm-up, goes
to its next phase as a Bridge Activity, and culminates in Activating
Material and Facilitation as Machine and Fluid Sculpting, both of
which are described in detail later in the book (see pp. 62 and 66).
The pieces can be used separately as they're described or as a
progression within one session. Any time you can use an activity
in the process and build on it in later activities it has two payoffs:
1) familiarity and comfort with the technique involved; and 2) a
sense of trust in how all the work relates to the larger picture of
what you hope to accomplish and address.

Trust Work

This series of activities focuses on the creation of ensemble—of going a step beyond playing together and working on comfort. These games begin to look at the feeling of community that a group can achieve even when working together in small and sometimes erratic doses. A safe space is developed through physical trust work, sensory work, and storytelling exercises designed to help individuals know each other in new and surprising ways. This stage of the process must follow the more playful, active games described earlier, because it is rarely appropriate to start a session with one of the activities in this series. People have to warm themselves up in the same space before they are ready to deepen the space as a group.

Tension, Laughter, and Focus

It is during these activities that you will be reminded how infrequently we human beings play together and connect with each other on simple, yet quite powerful levels. You will see some self-consciousness, fear, shyness, cynicism—and laughter. Especially laughter. When people get tense, for a million different reasons, their bodies look for release. Laughter accomplishes this and more. It's our strongest defense mechanism; we figure if we laugh first, no one can laugh at us.

Ensemble: At its simplest, a group of people that work together regularly. At its best, a group of people who work well together, trust one other, and depend upon each other.

I used to get frustrated when participants laughed. I knew that if someone laughed in a game, not only were they disrupting others, but they wouldn't be able to stay in scenes and in other work that we would eventually move toward. I would play the disciplinarian and try to force them into concentration. Sometimes it worked, more often it didn't, and we would both get frustrated. I later realized that the focus of each activity was key; not discipline for the sake of rules but, as I mentioned before, for focusing on the task at hand. Support, not scolding, and constant reminding that we had to accomplish certain things as a group before we could move to the next level was much more productive. I have had much greater success helping even the worst giggler find their focus in this manner. The most important thing is not to ignore it, but perhaps call out the need for better focus to the whole group rather than singling the one person out. Don't let it slide and assume it will take care of itself. It won't. Tension is natural. We have unfortunately been socialized out of play. Laughter is natural. It's our instinctual response for self-preservation. Concentration is natural also. It is, however, often out of practice and rusty. Nurture it, support it, and push it. In a safe space, watch the tension go away as the joy of the process takes over and the need for defensive laughter eventually disappears.

Trust Circle

Number of People: 7–9 per group (up to 5 groups in the space if there is room and if there is an adult or focused/trusted leader in each group)
Age Level: 13 and up
Time: 15–40 minutes
Source: Unknown

The Basic Idea

First, everyone must focus. Everyone stands in a circle with their eyes closed and puts their feet together, makes their body stiff like a board, and breathes. Then everyone leans forward with their body, still stiff, and tries to find the balance point where if they were to lean any further they would tip off-balance. Everyone holds that spot for about 15–20 seconds. Repeat the same thing leaning backward; then again to the left; and then to the right. Finally, everyone tries to connect those four points by making a circle with their whole body while their eyes are still closed. Repeat with a circle in the other direction and then return to center. Have everyone open their eyes but there should still be no talking.

Next, have 6–8 people form a tight circle around you. Everyone else forms a bigger circle around this circle and watches. You are demonstrating as the first participant so you're describing all of this as you do it. You put your feet together, arms crossed in an X over your chest, hands clenched in fists, eyes closed, and body stiff like a board. Everyone in the small circle has their hands up as if to brace the person in the center. When the small circle collectively says "ready," you let yourself fall forward. The person you fall toward and the two people on each side of them catch you. They place you back at center. They don't toss you across the circle. You let yourself fall again. After a couple of minutes someone in the small circle says "put them back to center." They do. Then someone says "move back if you want." Those who feel comfortable moving further from you do so. When they say "ready," you let yourself fall again. Another minute or two passes and someone says "put them back to center." You open your eyes and it's the next person's turn. At this point, the larger circle breaks into smaller groups and they begin to play, as demonstrated, with an adult or designated leader in each group. Each circle plays until everyone who wants to be in the center has had a chance. Afterward, you should process this activity.

Reminders
- It should be made very clear that no one has to get in the center. It should be said out loud that if someone doesn't want to be in the center it doesn't mean they don't trust the others in the circle. They simply don't want to do it. There are a number of people with touch issues for whom this game is very scary. Demand no explanation but offer the opportunity a couple of times throughout the game in case they change their mind. Allow people to say no, remain in the circle, and then gently check to see if anyone is thinking about trying it.
- The game should be silent. Other than "ready" and other instructions, it demands silence and concentration. It's not about scaring people but earning their trust. One joke, a giggle, or casual talk is much scarier than the feeling of weight shifting and people struggling to hold you.
- Each person is responsible for their own level of comfort regarding catching the center person. They should stand as close as they think they need to in order to support the weight and only move back if they are comfortable doing so. This is important.
- You will have to remind the center person to keep their body stiff and straight and their feet together otherwise they can be hard to catch and support.
- People don't hit the ground in this activity. If you set it up carefully, safely, and with focus, you're fine. It does help for the leader to go first.

Thoughts
This is a powerful activity if you work in a focused and nonpres-sured way. It involves touch, eyes closed, and teamwork. It demands a lot within an achievable doable structure. Don't make a big deal

out of anyone's trepidation. Simply reiterate that no one has to get in the center and then watch carefully how the most reluctant people respond as others try it and enjoy it. Let each person set their own boundaries. That's a very empowering thing. You can return to this at another time in your process and see how the group responds. This is not an activity to use until there is already a certain level of trust in the group. It's not a first day activity. I usually try it a third of the way into a process.

Trust Falls

Number of People: 8 or more
Age Level: 13 and up
Time: 5–10 minutes
Source: Unknown

The Basic Idea

Everyone finds a partner. One partner puts their feet together, closes their eyes, and holds their body stiff. The other person puts their hands on their partner's shoulder blades and says "ready." The person with their eyes closed falls backward to be supported by their partner. The supporting partner places them upright and moves their hands a few inches away from their partner's body. They say "ready" again and the blind partner allows their body to fall. The supporting partner continues to back up in small increments. They continue until either the partner with their eyes closed says "that's enough," meaning they don't want to fall any farther, or the sighted partner says "that's enough," meaning they can't support the fall from any farther. At that point, they reverse roles and begin again. When both partners have gone, they sit down and face each other. I always follow this activity with storytelling (described on p. 44).

Reminders

- It's not a contest to see who can fall farther or who is braver or stronger. It's important that everyone understands that this activity is about setting one's own boundaries and pushing oneself to participate at the same time.
- Make sure each pair has plenty of space.
- Participants shouldn't rush. If pairs finish before others they should quietly watch them finish.

Thoughts

I often do this right after the Trust Circle, moving from a group physical trust activity to a partner activity that demands more personal contact.

Blind (No Contact)

Number of People: 10 or more
Age Level: 13 and up
Time: 10–20 minutes
Source: Original

The Basic Idea

Create a rectangle of space using chairs or trash cans, much like in Cover the Space. There are two single-file lines of equal number facing each other. One line closes their eyes. To start, you will silently point at individuals in the other line. As they are pointed at, each individual will cross to the other line and take someone (not the person directly across from them) by the hand, or shoulder, or arm(s). They will begin to guide this person around the space, inside the rectangle. Their goal is to make sure that their partner does not touch (no contact at all) anyone during the game. As more pairs get into the space, the game gets more difficult and crowded. You complicate it by moving the corners and making the space smaller. You also take various moments to call out "faster," "slow motion," "only move backward," "crawl," and other challenges. You can also say "freeze" and ask the leader to take hold of their partner in a different way (by the hand, foot-to-foot, and so on). After a while, you say "freeze." Tell them to open their eyes and discuss the experience with their partner. Then process the activity with the whole group.

Variation

Instead of physically leading their partner, the sighted person crosses the space, finds a partner, makes a sound (nonword) and begins to repeat it. The sound becomes the cue that the blind partner follows. Rather than calling out different forms of movement or new holds, you call for the leading partner to move farther away from their partner and still guide their movement. A fascinating form of communication is often forced into the relationship. It can end by having the leaders move as far away in the space from their partner as possible and have all of them simultaneously try to guide their partner to them. Those who created a system of communication rather than just a sound generally succeed, and it's productive to talk about.

I don't recommend playing these two versions consecutively. Start with the first one and save this version for another time when you're looking for another trust work activity.

Reminders

- When you tell the line to close their eyes, remind them that no one will mess with them. They will hear all the instructions and they'll know exactly what's going on.
- You must have enough space to play this so it's dependent on your group size.
- Besides not allowing contact, the goal of the leading partner is to earn the trust of their partner. They should try to move smoothly and fluidly so they can work as a team and try more challenging movements as they develop a relationship and style of communication.
- The blind partner's challenge is to not just be led around and to turn their brain off, but to concentrate and try to find their partner's impulse of movement. They should feel when their partner is about to do something and move with him/her as opposed to after him/her. They should think of it as a dance rather than being on a leash.
- They should be silent throughout so that they don't know who their partner is and to maintain group concentration.

Thoughts

This is a game that I often use early in a process or in a one-shot session because it works on trust at a fairly basic level. It has people in physical contact with each other, sharing common goals, and protecting each other. It's interesting to hear what people have to say, particularly around the ideas of power and control, after this game. It's also interesting to explore their comfort level in either role (leader or follower) within the game. I often follow up this activity with Storytelling (described on p. 44).

I was at a conference conducting an all-day session for adults. I really enjoy those days because nobody knows what to expect. They come in thinking they'll sit down, get some handouts, and maybe do some kind of experiential activity. At this session, hardly anybody knew each other, and the room of participants started out being fairly uncomfortable. When we got to this activity, after two other warm-ups, the group took it very seriously. They focused and worked together extremely well. They played to accomplish the assigned task in a professional manner and the concentration and effort was palpable. When I finally told them to relax, open their eyes, and meet their partner, there was an explosive release of tension: laughter, conversation, and even hugs. The normal barriers of awkwardness melted in a collective moment of permission to be there, to just be there with other people and to connect. Those moments are wonderful and quite valuable in any group process.

Find Your Mother Like a Little Penguin

Number of People: 10 or more (must have an even number)
Age Level: 12 and up
Time: 10–20 minutes
Source: Boal

The Basic Idea

Everyone stands in a circle and numbers off by twos: 1, 2, 1, 2, etc. The 1s step out in front of the person to their right, face them, and make a sound with their mouth (not a word) that they can repeat over and over again without giggling. The 2 that is listening memorizes the sound. The 1s return to their place in the circle. Then the 2s step out in front of the person to their right, face them, and make a sound (a different one) with their mouth that they can repeat over and over without giggling. The 1 that is listening memorizes the sound. The 2s take their place back in the circle. Everyone closes their eyes and takes the hand of the person on each side of them. They have 15 seconds to memorize the feel of the hands. Their eyes remain closed for the duration of the game.

Then you explain how the game will be played: When you say "go," everyone in the room will slowly and carefully begin to mix themselves up in the space so they don't know where they are or who they are near. Then, you'll say "freeze." After a few seconds of silence, you'll say "Find your mother like a little penguin." Everyone will start making their sound while slowly moving around. Everyone is listening for the sound made by the person who was originally standing to their left. When they find them, they take that person's right hand, clasp it, make sure it's the correct hand, and hold onto it. Each person is searching for the person who was standing to their left while each person is being searched for by the person who was standing to their right. Slowly, the circle puts itself back together. Before saying "go," have them all make their sound one last time so they can hear what they'll be seeking one more time. Then, the game can begin.

Reminders

- They can't make their sound too soft (or it won't be heard) or too loud (or they'll drown out other sounds).
- When their right hand is clasped, they have been found and they should stop making their sound so others still searching will have less difficulty.
- They are putting a circle together, not straight lines, so they need to keep moving. If they get stuck, they should work their way down the links of the line to try and find their "mother."
- If their right hand is empty they should keep making their sound.
- They need to stay silent and to not laugh. The tension and concentration, as well as the teamwork involved, gives the game its spark. You may need to help them with that.

Thoughts

This is a fun and challenging game. Take your time setting it up. I use it about halfway to two-thirds of the way into a process. A certain level of trust is necessary for a group to engage in it and feel like they can actually accomplish the goal, especially with larger groups. Groups do succeed almost all of the time, and if not, it's a great chance to talk about what did or didn't happen. There is a wonderful sense of achievement upon completion and a nice opportunity to discuss frustration and the process if some didn't enjoy it as much. Throughout, encourage everyone to stay in it and not give up. Remember: task-related discipline and focus.

Glass Cobra

Number of People: 10 or more
Age Level: 12 and up
Time: 10–20 minutes
Source: Boal

The Basic Idea

Everyone starts walking around the space without talking or contact. After a few minutes everyone stands in a circle and closes their eyes. You rearrange them, placing them in a new circle so they don't know who is next to them. Their eyes will stay closed for the remainder of the game. Everyone turns to their right and puts their hands on the shoulders of the person in front of them. They have 20 seconds to memorize the back of that person's neck, hair, collar, and so on. There should be no tickling, just a quick, respectful inventory. Then they drop their hands. When you say "go," they slowly and carefully mix themselves up around the room. Then you say "freeze," pause, "put the cobra together and find your tail." They put the circle back together by finding the person whose back they memorized.

Reminders

- The game is silent the whole time.
- Some people don't like to have their necks touched. Watch your group. If you sense someone is real uncomfortable help them out. It's rare but I have had a couple folks step out of this.
- The searching must be gentle, nonaggressive, nontickling, and respectful. It's not groping.
- They must remember that they are forming a circle not a straight line.

Thoughts

This is an easier game to play than Find Your Mother Like a Little Penguin, but because it requires a larger degree of touch, I usually play it later in the process. This is often a relaxed and comfortable activity. Without going overboard on touch awareness, it's important to be sensitive to boundaries and constantly watch the dynamics of the group. All of these eyes-closed group activities are great to process afterward. A lot of observations and feelings are often shared.

Circle Height

Number of People: 10 or more
Age Level: 8 and up
Time: 10–20 minutes
Source: Original

The Basic Idea

Everyone mixes up in the space with their eyes closed. You say "freeze." When you say "go," each person begins searching and places themselves according to height in a circle with the shorter person on the left and the taller person on the right. When a person believes they have found their place in the circle they should keep hold of each person's hand. Ultimately, the tallest person in the group should end up with the shortest person in the group on the right. This is a silent game.

Reminders

- They need to respect each other as they search for their place in the circle.
- Remind them they're making a circle not a straight line.

Create your own variations on these eyes-closed, group circle games. They are powerful and can take on a sense of ritual in the structure of your sessions if you use them often. Groups enjoy them because they demand focus and bring a bit of magic and newness to the space and the day.

Thoughts

This game sounds nonthreatening, especially with big groups. It allows participants to feel safe with their eyes closed as they focus on a seemingly simple task. You're just asking them to make a circle from shortest to tallest. If you have created a relaxed space that is energized and safe the group ends up having a miniadventure with their eyes closed. You will get a sense here of how task-related discipline is developing. If the group works to accomplish this seemingly simple yet specific task, you learn that their ensemble building is moving forward. If they half-heartedly go through the motions, you learn that you need to work harder to build the ensemble.

Falling

Number of People: 10 or more
Age Level: 13 and up
Time: 10–20 minutes
Source: Original

The Basic Idea

You mark out a rectangle in the space using chairs or trash cans (as in Cover The Space); the area marked out should be large enough for everyone to walk around without feeling jammed in, but small enough that no one can ever be too far away from others. Everyone starts silently walking around with no contact. Everyone continues to walk around as you become the first one to demonstrate and explain what will happen next. Once the game starts anyone can stop in their place, shout out "falling," and let themselves fall backward, keeping their body stiff as a board. Upon hearing the word "falling," everyone else, no matter where they are in the space, tries to get to that person. By the time the person is actually falling, half the group has gotten there to catch them. When the group catches the person, they gently place them upright and return to the game. The trick is the person has to stop, say "falling," and then fall. That vocalization allows people to start moving *before* the actual fall. It's also crucial that they fall toward the middle of the space. You go first then allow the game to find its own pace. If there are periods of time when no one falls, that's okay. Trust the game to find itself. If you've created a safe space and you are at least halfway into your process, it will happen.

Variation

Once the person is caught, the group gently lets them all the way down to the ground. Then the person gets up and the game continues.

Reminders

• This is not a game to joke around in. Focus is important for it to be safe.

- The game is silent except when the person says "falling."
- No one has to elect to fall.
- Everyone has to make the effort to be there and catch the falling person.
- Listen to each other. If two people call "falling" at once (which is rare), get to the body nearest you.
- After a person is caught, the group gently places them upright and continues moving about the space.

Thoughts

This is a wonderful ensemble building game that feels scary at first and is soon generally quite popular. Don't let enthusiasm distract from focus, especially since safety is involved. Remind everyone that the goal is almost a hyperaware state of preparedness where all senses are in tune to the people and movement in the space. This activity makes concrete the idea of high stakes, which you will later spend time developing in fictional situations with your group. You can refer back to this game, an instant when a task they all shared had very high stakes, and ask them to remember what their bodies felt like when they were truly engaged, ready, and active. That means you need to help them be engaged, ready, and active with a certain level of relaxed intensity during this activity.

Storytelling

Number of People: Any number (preferably an even number)
Age Level: Any age (though it's different with children under 12 years old)
Time: 10–20 minutes
Source: Original

The Basic Idea

Everyone chooses a partner. (I do this activity after a physical, partner activity, like Trust Falls or Blind (No Contact), and then simply have the partners sit down and face each other.) Then, you talk about the power of stories to turn issues and facts into people and lives; about the connection between theatre and stories; and about the questions "What is a story?" and "What does it mean to tell a story?" As you move on with your work, the group will use truth and fiction to explore things that matter to them. Here is a chance to safely begin. Each person will have 3–5 minutes (you decide) to tell a true story to their partner about themselves and a topic you give them. When you call out to switch, it's the other partner's turn. Not before. For this activity, a story has a beginning, middle, and end; is filled with details; and means something to the teller. Topics might include trust, fear, love, an apology, a discovery, a recent challenge, or any of a million things general enough that will call up lots of responses, but specific enough to share a tone or starting point. There is no *wrong* story; whatever subject comes to the person that they want to divulge is okay.

Reminders

- The goal here is not to tell a deep, dark, personal, rip-your-guts-out secret story. It is to tell a story you are comfortable about and at ease with sharing, especially the first time this activity takes place. This is important. It's not about seeing who can reveal the most or shred their emotions publicly. Each person takes care of themselves.
- A story is an event and the relationships and circumstances that surround it. It is not a string of facts, and it is not my entire history with my parents. It is contained, and it is rich with specificity.

- If someone finishes their story before you call out "switch," they should start over and fill in details: the clothes, the weather, the smells, the human context. Prod them to do this. The details of human interaction here lays the groundwork for the specifics they will need to create stories and scenes later.
- This is most effective with folks who don't know each other well. But if they do, challenge them to tell each other new stories and to know each other in fresh, new ways. Stay on them about not lapsing into familiarity.
- Everyone should know that their story is just between them and their partner. They will not be asked to share it with the rest of the group.

Thoughts

This activity is an important step in group building and in the process of going deeper with this work. It begins to bring together topics, imagination (in the form of memory and structure of the story), and the contextualization of the way people relate to each other and the actions they take. Later, you can shift into stories more directly related to issues being explored, such as moments of decision and pressures. It's good stuff and if you build it into the process and take your time with it, it pays off.

One afternoon I was in a planning session with a group I had just trained. That evening we were conducting an open performance workshop for community members around issues of parent/child communication. We were discussing the structure of the upcoming session. I said I wanted to use Storytelling to lead from the warm-ups into the bridge activity and to introduce the topic for the first time. One of the youth said she felt that although Storytelling was useful in training, it was too much to ask of a group together for the first time. She felt it required a higher level of trust than we could count on that night. I politely disagreed, saying that if you set up group rules and a safe space, everyone will find a level at which they can be comfortable telling a story. We had a good discussion and tried the activity that night. It brought us closer as a group and freed up plenty of issues in the minds of the participants. Rarely is there a wrong time for this activity.

Tour of a Place

Number of People: Any number (preferably an even number)
Age Level: All ages
Time: 20–30 minutes
Source: Unknown (Taught to me by Trish Suchy in a writing workshop)

The Basic Idea

Everyone gets a partner, closes their eyes, and thinks of an actual physical place (a room, a building, a forest, an island, a church, a playground) that is very special to them. Each person pictures their place in great detail down to the color of the curtains or the texture of the grass. Everyone opens their eyes. Then each person takes their partner on a five to ten minute (you decide) guided tour of that place, actually walking through the space you are in, but describing the physical specifics of their memory in absolute detail. The trick is for them to only describe the physical layout without sharing stories that happened in that space. If the person getting toured asks a question (e.g., "How did that hole get there?," "Did you ever come out here with anyone else?," or "What was the first time you came here like?"), the guide can respond with a story. Together, they have to find a balance whereby the whole place gets toured and some stories get shared. When time is up, you call "switch," and the other partner conducts a tour.

Reminders

- They must move around, not just stand and talk. This can be the first venture into an imaginary space, and the feeling of their bodies actively moving through that imaginary space can be recalled in later work.
- The tour guide should not describe the space in a clinical way, but rather relate the emotional importance of this space. This introduces the idea of making something not actually present important to them in the present moment. It is pretend with truth to jump-start the emotion. The truth is it's a real space in their life, past or present, and they have the task to make someone else see it.

- If someone finishes early, they should be coaxed into describing the space in greater detail. The "tourist" can also help by asking more questions.

Thoughts

I don't couple this with a physical partner activity. I think of this as an activity on its own.

Session Planning

As you pull other games into your planning, consider your own understanding of why and where you will use them in the overall structure of this process. Remember the keys to creating a plan for your own use: *your goals, the time frame,* and *the building blocks,* rather than random activities used in random places. I have laid out some sample sessions I have used for working with various structures in Appendix B, which I hope will be helpful guides and springboards.

Bridge Work

Bridge activities are the link between the warm-ups and the activating material. Their goal is to theatricalize the space; that is, to take advantage of the energy generated during the warm-ups and to begin focusing on imagination and issues. Bridge activities use image work, improvisation, and discussion to create pretend worlds, explore group perceptions, and start to identify core issues for dialogue. The activities are varied and, unlike warm-ups, many can be replayed with entirely different aims and experiences. Some of these options will be explored here but you should look for and expect to find ways to use this work in ways not mentioned.

I recently worked with a teacher who was finding cultural differences among her older teen students a roadblock to concentration and trust. She wanted to move forward as an ensemble and explore stories to perform but found that group tension and anger constantly prevented her going as far as she wanted in sessions. After we spoke at length, she began to use image work as a bridge focusing on those same cultural and language differences that she had been trying to avoid. She found passion, excitement, and drama in her group as the safe structure of nonverbal theatre work engaged the participants where they lived, so to speak. It opened up channels through which they could process the issues in activating material they began to create together. Bridge work is the nonjarring transition work that makes the process more than role playing, more than a step-by-step curriculum. It establishes an atmosphere that is theatrical, nurturing, and all about dialogue; it takes forethought and creative energy to incorporate and integrate it. Use it.

Bridge work is crucial to the process described in this book. It is also the part most often left out and the seemingly hardest part to plan. Often, in a group process using theatre, a leader will warm the group up and then because of time constraints, jump right into some form of activating work. Bridge work allows the energy generated in the warm-ups to gently become creative and quietly begins to address subjects of interest and concern to the participants. It makes the space safer, it engages the imagination, and it theatricalizes the setting. The activities described in this section take your work deeper. Make them part of your daily work and build them into your long-term arc. In particular, the image work and machine work is flexible and can be used in many ways. Allow yourself the freedom to clarify what you want to focus on and accomplish; play with these activities.

Note: Some of the activities in this section are improvisation-based. There is a separate section dealing with improvisation exercises to help your group deepen its work and prepare for scenes. The improvisation exercises are listed here because their main goal is not skill building but to bridge the energy from warm-ups to creating activating material. Do not hesitate to use these particular activities as bridges before working specifically on improvisation skills.

Environment

Number of People: 8 or more
Age Level: All ages
Time: 15–45 minutes
Source: Original via Spolin and Living Stage

The Basic Idea

The group sits facing as large an open space as possible. A volunteer enters the space and begins doing an activity that would take place in a specific location. For instance, he/she begins to wait on a table, and those watching realize the space is a restaurant. They cannot mouth words. They are focusing on an activity or a series of activities and making that action real. As soon as someone knows where the activity is taking place, they enter the space and begin doing another activity that could also take place in that location. People keep entering the space until, ideally, everyone is in the space by the end of the round. There is no talking and no interacting with each other. Everyone is silently focused on the physical world and activity they are creating in that same space. After a short period of time, they freeze, relax, and play another round.

Variations

Circumstance: You can play with circumstance: "It's raining"; "The power has gone out"; or "Everyone remembers they forgot to do something very important. What do you do now?" You are asking them to quickly make imaginary situations important and real.

Character: You can add the focus of character so that you talk them through specific character choices as they carry out their actions. For instance, you could say "How old are you?," "What do you do for a living?," "Where do you live?" to help them build a person and a story. Then, you can freeze them and say, "It's 10:00 A.M. on a Friday morning—where are you and what are you doing? Do it." Everyone creates an environment and activity based on who they are. The space then becomes a variety of places. You can take them through a whole day like this and keep asking them questions about their lives. After the exercise you can have a great conversation about how character can generate story, how specifics can lead to all sorts of interesting discoveries, and how generalities can be dead ends.

Issues: To bring issues in later in the process, you could say, "Each of your characters is visiting someone in the hospital. Who and why? Do it." Or "Alcohol has created some situation you have to deal with right now. What is it and where are you? Go." You can generate issues with the group and randomly use them over time.

I recently saw an interview with Dennis Hopper on a television show and he was asked about his friendship with James Dean. The questions eventually led to Dean's impact on Hopper's acting. Hopper said Dean's only main advice was: "Stop showing. You're showing everything. Don't show it. Do it. DO IT! If you're drinking, drink. If you're listening, listen. If you're trying to get someplace, get there. That's real. People care about that." Hopper said that, although he has his own system and way of working, that's his guiding principle. Always. I knew I liked James Dean for good reason.

Combinations: Combining these different variations you can create new and interesting ways to challenge and engage participants.

Reminders
- This activity—like all of them—is not about entertaining an audience. It's not about performing but focusing on the task at hand and creating imaginary worlds. Don't let them turn it into comedy or showboating. THE RULE (for this game and for acting in general): Don't show. DO!
- Encourage participants to create environments where lots can happen.
- If someone starts in a space, it's actually the entire space. They don't have to feel stuck in the one room the first person creates (e.g., if someone starts in a classroom, the space can be the whole school).

Thoughts
This is an easy activity to use when you simply want to make a smooth transition to imagination work without engaging in issues too much. It's fun, and although it requires a lot of focus, the array

of variations allows you to return to it and watch it pay off. The focus on location and character makes it an excellent activity to use to develop your group's improvisational skills. Groups that train to lead performance workshops with peers often use this game as a bridge with their participants.

Values Clarification

Number of People: 8 or more
Age Level: All ages (You make the statements age appropriate.)
Time: 20–60 minutes
Source: Original via Teen AIDS Prevention curriculum written by Advocates for Youth

The Basic Idea

Everyone sits in one part of the room facing the largest open space. You stand and explain the game, which includes making the reminders clear (in the beginning and throughout the game). You put down signs in different areas that say Agree, Unsure, and Disagree. Everyone will listen as you read a statement (some sample statements follow). Each person decides how they feel and moves to that sign. You stand in the center and give people in each group a chance to say why they made that choice. After everyone who wanted to share their thoughts has had a chance, you read the next statement.

Reminders

- The goal of this activity is to ask everyone to think about the subject matter in the statements, begin to feel comfortable sharing their point of view in the group, and learn about other people's points of view.
- This activity is about being nonjudgmental, listening, and agreeing to disagree. It is about respecting the fact that different people see things differently. If you are lucky, there will be a range of opinions on many of the statements.
- The BIG RULE to keep this from being a debate or feeling unsafe is that no one can respond to anyone else's opinion. They can only respond to the statement that was read. If they start to respond to someone's opinion or disagree with someone directly, you remind them that it's not appropriate. If they continue, you tell them "thank you," and go on to

someone else. It is important that you make it very clear that you won't tolerate a moment of the space feeling unsafe during this activity.

- Folks can move to another choice while people are expressing their opinion if they change their mind.
- No one has to speak. In the interest of time, people shouldn't repeat each other. Opinions should be brief so that everyone who wants to can speak. Remember people can say "pass" or "it's been said."
- Have the smallest group discuss their choice last. If only a few people are in a group and they go first, they will feel odd or worse when a big group discusses their choice at the end. I always let the small group finish and I explain why.
- Don't just rattle off these reminders; make sure they are understood. Discuss them.
- Generate statements with your group. That is often the most productive part of this activity.

Thoughts

This is a wonderful activity to practice listening and hearing. Talk about the difference between those two words.

I have seen some peer groups use this activity as an energy builder to provoke conflict and jump-start a workshop with peers. This is a huge mistake. It sets up animosity and creates a negative space. Use it safely and as a way to pave the road for healthy dialogue, not to activate a provocative dialogue. If you get honest responses here your dialogue later will be much stronger.

As you move into sessions where you're working with scenes, you will find using this as a bridge activity with statements that relate to the issues of that day's scene can be exciting.

Some facilitators choose to participate in this. Some choose to stand out but welcome questions as to how they would respond. Some find it important to their teaching/leading status that they pass completely. It's your call.

Sample Statements

These are some statements some groups have used. The wording is tricky, because they need to be specific but they also need to leave room for interpretation. In my mind, a good statement is one which puts some people in the room in each group.

I am worried that I, or someone I love, will get AIDS.

I think that sexual intercourse is appropriate only between married people.

I would stop a friend who was drunk or high from having sex at a party.

I would feel uncomfortable eating food prepared by a person with AIDS.

I think it should be a crime for a person who is HIV+ to have sexual intercourse without telling their partner.

It is a person's responsibility to urge a friend with an eating disorder to seek help.

Homosexual marriages should be legalized.

It is OK to drink to get drunk.

Marijuana usually leads to the use of harder drugs.

Parents and their children should talk about sex.

I am comfortable with my body.

Sometimes violence is the only option.

I contribute to the atmosphere that allows eating disorders to occur.

I see discrimination in our community.

Two Revelations

Number of People: 6 or more
Age Level: 11 and up
Time: 15–30 minutes
Source: Boal

The Basic Idea

Everyone gets a partner. They stand together in their own space as you have them make the following decisions together, one decision at a time. You give them about 15 seconds for each one.

Who will be the parent and who will be the child?

How old is each of them? (They can choose for the child to be between the age of the youngest in the room to a couple of years older than the oldest youth present.)

Where will the scene take place?

Who will enter the scene and who will start in the space?

The following part shouldn't be discussed between partners. They make these decisions secretly.

Each partner has to come up with a secret. It should be an extremely important, realistic secret that they think a parent might keep from a child or a child might keep from a parent, depending on who they are playing. It should be a secret that they think someone might realistically keep in their community. It's a big deal but not "soap opera, fakey." It could happen.

Then they each come up with a reason why they have to tell the other person the secret in this scene. (HINT: What do they need from the other person?)

When you say "go," the person who is starting in the space begins to do an activity that could take place in that space (cooking in a kitchen, for instance); the other person enters, and the scene starts. They talk. Perhaps one of them blurts their secret out. Perhaps there is small talk. The catch is that when the first one says their secret, the second person cannot say theirs until the game leader shouts "second revelation, go!" Together they have to deal with the first secret while the other person has theirs still churning around in their gut. The scene continues for a while after the second secret is revealed, then you shout "freeze, relax" and everyone comes together to process.

Reminders

- This is an improvisation game to play before working on improv skills.
- They should concentrate on listening to each other.
- They should concentrate on making the relationship real.
- They should work to stay focused and not fall out of the scene (e.g., giggle, look around). Everyone does this at once so there is no audience.
- They should make the secrets important to them so these are not casual conversations but events and confrontations that mean something to these characters.

Thoughts

This game accomplishes two great things. First, it gives you a sense of how comfortable your group is with improvisation and scene work. You can get a sense of how focused they are by just watching them play with each other in an intense situation. This will help you determine where you are in the process in terms of skills and group building even before you've worked specifically on improv. Second, it asks your group "what are the secrets people—families in particular—keep from each other in this community?" It is a powerful and subtle way to discover how those in the room view communication and "taboo" topics in the home. With the group, talk about secrets that appeared in more than one scene and about those that didn't come up. This is an important activity to process and listen to. Not the details of each scene per se but the content of what was and wasn't said. Generalize through these specific fictions and see what you learn. Also, it can be played again later but between a different relationship (friends, siblings, and so on).

I was in a small town playing this game once, and when we processed the secrets, everyone playing the child had a secret about pregnancy and everyone playing the parent had a secret about infidelity. The group was composed of twelve teens and four adults. When this came to light they were fairly stunned. It led to a fascinating discussion on secrets in the community, and it set the agenda for the initial issue work we did. It came out of creative activity, not talk. This made it more potent, more real, and more felt.

Complete the Image

Number of People: 6 or more
Age Level: All ages
Time: 15–40 minutes
Source: Boal

The Basic Idea

Everyone sits down together and faces the largest open space in the room. You ask two volunteers to come up front. They shake hands, look at each other, and you shout "freeze." They must freeze their position, including their facial expression, and prepare to hold it for a while. You turn out to the group and ask them what they see. There are two human beings but what else is going on in that image, in that moment, between those two people? There are no wrong answers so try to get as many interpretations as you can. You might ask what relationships they see. What relationships they don't see. What the story is in this situation.

There are no wrong answers in image work, because every image holds truth for its creator. Therefore, all responses are "right." Freeing up your group to realize that and to act on it is a constant and wonderful goal.

Then, you relax one of the frozen people and let them sit down. The other person stays frozen, and you ask someone else in the group to come up and to create a new image by placing themselves in a position in relation to the already frozen person. They can be touching the already frozen person or be completely separate. The two bodies create a new image together. Once the second person has found their place they freeze. Once again, you ask the group what they see. You relax the original person in the image, and he/she sits down. A new person comes in. The same thing occurs. You do this three or four times, then have one person go out, and you explain how the rest of the game will work.

At this point, you can demonstrate by using the group member still up there and a new one, or you can demonstrate by taking the role of the second person in the image yourself and explaining the next phase as you actually do it. I always do the latter. I find it breaks the ice nicely.

You explain that after the demonstration everyone in the room is going to get a partner and do what they've just seen. Two people shake hands, look at each other, and freeze (as shown in the first part of this activity). One of them unfreezes, looks at their frozen partner, and takes a new position. Then, the other person unfreezes, looks at their frozen partner, and takes a new position. This keeps repeating so it's a constant flow: both frozen; one unfreezes, looks, adds back in; both frozen for two or three seconds; the other unfreezes; and so on. The demonstration should go on for at least two minutes in silence after it's explained to help establish focus, silence, and the variety of images people can create. The images might be realistic or they might be abstract. They might come from the head or they might be gut responses. The pair continues to have this structured dialogue of images. The group breaks into partners and plays for five to fifteen minutes. You can call out a theme or idea (such as communication, jealousy, family) and ask them to allow the word to influence their playing together. If the word starts restricting them, they should ignore it. It's there to add a layer, or it should disappear. After a while you say "freeze, relax," and everyone comes together to process.

Reminders
- The whole process should be silent.
- Encourage them to use the space (the floor, any walls or doorways) and not to get stuck with two people standing near each other.
- Remind them their face is a large part of the images they create.
- They shouldn't worry about what they look like. There is no audience. Everyone is playing.

Thoughts
This is the first image theatre activity I put in the process. In addition to the variations on Sculpting, Complete the Image engages participants in nonverbal dialogue. It is theatrical in an unusual, powerful, and freeing way. It is also simple to play and if you have succeeded at establishing some focus and trust, the intensity with which a group may take to this work will surprise you. It allows participants to create together with no burdens of right or wrong, or even trying to communicate to others. It is a wonderful bridge because it uses the body, exercises the imagination, and if it touches on issues (adding the words), it does so in a safe and abstract way.

Sculpting

Number of People: 6 or more
Age Level: All ages
Time: 15–60 minutes
Source: Original via Living Stage

The Basic Idea

Phase 1: Everyone sits in a circle and you brainstorm about the issue(s) you will be exploring with the group. For example, you can ask the group to share thoughts or concerns they have regarding violence among their peers and in their community. You can either go around the circle or call on hands. People talk. It's not a dialogue at this point. People briefly say what's on their mind and others listen.

After hearing the thoughts and concerns just shared, you ask the group for single words that come to mind around this issue. These can be topics, themes, emotions (i.e., fear, relationship, anger, guns, crime, gangs, jealousy, race, harassment, home). You write them down as they're called out. Aim for a list of 30–50 single words. Without letting it go on too long, you finish making the list and read it back to them. This list will serve as a blueprint for the rest of this activity, but it is also one that you'll be able to return to again and again.

Phase 2 (Partner Sculpt): Demonstrate to the group how to sculpt human clay. The sculptor can sculpt by touching the clay and moving them into place or by mirroring and showing them the position they should take. The sculptor cannot talk. The entire activity is completely silent. Everyone gets a partner. One partner will start as the sculptor, the other as clay. You call out a word from the list and the sculptor uses the clay to create an image in response to the word, to make a piece of art. The goal is not to illustrate the word or to play charades. It is to shape, imagine, and create. The image can be realistic, abstract, concrete, or symbolic. THERE ARE NO WRONG ANSWERS OR IMAGES! It doesn't have to have a "meaning" the sculptor wants to communicate. It can come from a gut response, thoughts, or just a feeling. After the sculptor has sculpted, they can walk around and look at others' images. There should be a gallery of responses to the word. When every sculptor has returned to their image you say "clay, relax" and the clay and sculptor trade places. You go back and forth through a variety of words until you feel ready to move on to Phase 3.

Phase 3 (Group Sculpt): Everyone gets into groups of four, five, or six. They pick someone to sculpt first. You call out a word and they sculpt. This time they have more pieces of clay to work with; just because they have more bodies, they don't have to sculpt a realistic story or scene. They can, but they can also still sculpt abstract images. They have to sculpt quickly and must still work silently. During each round of words you can relax all the images but one and allow everyone to see each other's work. You go around the room until each image has been featured and then move to the next word. You want to make sure each group member has a chance to sculpt at least once before moving on to Phase 4.

> *The sculptor should sculpt quickly. Go with an idea; don't agonize over the perfect image. This keeps the activity moving and reinforces that all interpretations are "right."*

Phase 4 (Circle Sculpt): Everyone stands in a circle and three people get in the middle. You call out a word from the list and these three people create an image on their own. They are all clay and they simply find a position in relation to each other as you count to 5. On "5" you call out "freeze" and they hold whatever position they are in. At this point you explain to the rest of the group that they are looking at one out of a billion possible images for this word. They will now have a chance to resculpt that image as much as they like. Anyone can step into the circle and resculpt. One at a time, the group tries to share as many images as they can. They sculpt silently and pause a few seconds between images. This continues until you stop the round and go on to a new word.

Variations on Processing

I like to let the images rest in silence and not talk about them much. Here are some ways you can verbally process the images, especially in Phases 3 and 4, if you choose to do so.

- If you want to talk about an image, ask what people see. Whatever responses they give are valuable. Make a point of not trying to have them answer in a certain context. Just ask what they see. Never have the person who sculpted say what they were trying to communicate or what the image means to them. That lives in the image, and if they speak it they nullify the million other interpretations in the room.
- Ask everyone who they think the main character is. Then, put your hand over each person's head in the image and ask everyone to imagine your hand as a thought bubble in a cartoon. As your hand is over each person, ask those watching to call out what would be in the bubble. Get as many ideas as possible.
- Have people tell the story they see in the image. Push for as many different stories as you can get.

Again, I like the power of the nonverbal dialogue that image work allows, but if you want to verbalize don't look for right and wrong or definitive. Just pull out responses.

Reminders
- Be a stickler for *absolute* silence throughout all phases of this activity, and in particular, when participants switch from being sculptors to being clay. It does away with self-consciousness and allows stillness to be seen and appreciated.
- Realize that focus will be tough at first. It feels strange to sculpt at the beginning. You want to allow some time the first time you do it to stay with it until the focus deepens. You can later come back to it in smaller time chunks.
- While circle sculpting, your group may sculpt for a minute or two and then appear done. Don't get scared by the silence, verbal or physical. Wait the pause out. Let the group know they are all participants, not spectators, and if they find themselves relaxed and watching, they should jump in and sculpt. Remind them that to not sculpt is a choice also. Nothing here is passive. They (and you) will eventually grow comfortable with the pauses. The work following a pause is often very interesting.
- As they walk around and look at images remind them to see

the images, not just glance at them. What similarities do they see between images? What differences? What response do they have to each image? The images are three-dimensional so they should move around and take them in from a variety of angles. How do the images change with the viewpoint?

- While sculpting, use the space. Place bodies on the floor, in doorways, by windows, and use distance and closeness. Don't just have upright bodies as clay. Lay them down. Intertwine them. Experiment with form as well as content.

Thoughts

Sculpting is my favorite technique. There's not been a session I've done where it couldn't be used in some way. It's fun. It's intense. It's revealing. It asks human beings to communicate in a way that is not common but is not foreign either. It bridges language and cultural barriers and sets up possibilities that can lead to all sorts of other activities. (I have used it with non-English speaking populations and with youths who are deaf.) Once a group knows it, it can be returned to again and again. It is always new and always powerful.

Machine

Number of People: Any number
Age Level: All ages
Time: 10–30 minutes
Source: Original via Spolin

The Basic Idea

This starts out like the warm-up version. Do one or two of the basic machines here to remind the group of the mechanics and to get them used to finding the group rhythm again. Then, say you're taking the activity in a different direction. There are two phases to this activity.

Phase 1: Create an emotion or theme machine. For instance, a fear machine. First, it's a standard silent machine with a twist: everyone's movement should come from a response to or feeling of fear. So the pieces are all different manifestations of physicalized fear. Each piece could be a figure causing fear, feeling fear, either abstract or concrete. There are no wrong answers. Once the machine is up and moving, you ask it to find its sound. You can have each person find a sound or you can have the whole machine find a collective sound of fear, slowly and together. The machine should start silently and add the sounds once it's moving. This can be a powerful and bonding creative act when played with focus. Other potential emotions or themes are apology, joy, guilt, love, shame, anger, envy.

Phase 2: Create a human machine around a topic. For instance, an alcohol machine. Again, it's a standard machine but the pieces are human beings involved in a situation or sharing a perspective around alcohol. People enter with a movement and a phrase or sentence they will repeat over and over. Some examples: "Just one more"; "That's enough, OK"; "What else are we going to do?"; "You want to go upstairs?" When the machine is up and full you can freeze and talk with the group about who (which characters) the voices belong to, what the situations and stories might be, and process the thoughts that have been expressed around the particular topic.

Reminders

- As with the warm-up activity, use the space, use the whole body; get everyone involved.
- Have the group look for all sides—contrasting as well—of the themes and topics you work from. Don't repeat voices and perspectives. Search for ones not yet found.

Thoughts

The topic machine is a great way to find ideas and characters in an active, imaginative way. It combines physicality and spontaneous creativity to actually produce an in-the-moment read of the group's thoughts around an issue without doing too much thinking. The voices created cannot only be processed but used to create activating scene work later on in the section on activating material. You can use topics, themes, or emotions that you come up with yourself or, as with Sculpting, generate the words with your group.

Monologue Work

Number of People: 6 or more
Age Level: All ages (topic specific)
Time: 30–45 minutes (to begin with)
Source: Original

The Basic Idea

First, you get a piece of poster board or an easel and you write YES and NO at the top. Then, with your group, you are going to generate a list under each heading. The base question comes from an issue you are exploring. Three examples:

1. Why do teens choose to be sexually active (YES) or to not be sexually active (NO)?
2. Why do teens chooses to use drugs (YES) or not to use drugs (NO)?
3. Why do teens choose to join gangs (YES) or not to join gangs (NO)?

Your list is a list of reasons. It can be words or phrases—brief thoughts on specific reasons why young people might make either choice. After making the list, every person picks a reason off the list (publicly, so there are no repeats) from either YES or NO and goes off and creates a character, point of view, and story that goes along with that reason. Each person spends ten minutes alone, thinking about who this person might be and creating a fictional story of a time when their choice was made for this reason.

Then, people come up one at a time, sit in a chair facing the group, and tell their story. They don't perform it. They simply tell it from the point of view of the character they've created. After they tell their story they stay in character and the rest of the group interviews them about their life, their choices, and their story. The group cannot be judgmental but they can be inquisitive and try to learn as much about this person and their point of view as they can. Then the next person goes. If you have a large group you could take time and go through everyone, or do one or two each session.

Note: If they ask, participants can write things down as they prepare their character and story, but they can't bring anything up front with them. Don't give this as an option at the beginning. Ideally, they're walking around and organizing their thoughts with their bodies.

Reminders
- The characters should be fictional, not someone they know. The story and person should be pulled from their own knowledge of the reality of the issue, their imagination, and their observation of human behavior.
- Have them pick a reason and create a character different than themselves. They should move away from their own feelings, strive to find a point of view they can't see themselves having, and make it real.
- Tell them to not just sit and think during the ten minutes of prep time: Create details, background, and a history of the character's life; discover how they are different; walk around, finding the way this person might move. How does their character's family life relate to the story they tell?
- The interview must be nonjudgmental. Hopefully, some participants will have created characters whose choices will make them unpopular, harsh, and even disliked. These characters are not to be brutalized through interrogation or raked over the coals to prove how "wrong" their decisions were in order to make them realize what they did to others and have them see the light. They should be questioned about their interactions, their decisions, the consequences—anything. But not judged and counseled. That's not what this activity is about.
- Remind participants of the storytelling activities they have done with each other. Beginning, middle, and end. Stories with detail and meaning for the teller. How can they invest these fictitious stories with the same simple qualities of significance and connection that the real stories had? Talk about this after each story and interview. What seems real? What doesn't? Why?

Thoughts
The monologues have a lot of levels going on at once. The storyteller is working on character, communication, clarity, emotional investment, and specific choices. (Some of these terms become clearer in

the next section on improvisation.) The listeners are actively listening and analyzing what they hear to discover and explore choices and issues they care about from one individual's perspective. They are forced to be nonjudgmental, to practice agreeing to disagree, and to respect others with different thoughts and values—and even to learn from other thoughts and values. These characters and stories can also be used to create scene work described later in Activating Material.

This Work Is Therapeutic—It Is *Not* Therapy!

There is no doubt that intense feelings and responses will sometimes arise as you do this work with youths and adults. The issues being explored will inevitably touch the life experience of someone in the room. The meaning for them, possibly for the whole group, may take on greater significance or emotional charge in these moments. That's OK. The key is to remember this work steers away from being psychodrama specific to any one individual because you are not trying to use a group to work through one person's problems. You are using a group to explore a social problem compressed into a specific, fictional interaction that is culled from the collective consciousness of the participants you are working with. The stories they tell and create may be the absolute experience of someone present but you are not shining a spotlight on a single "true-life" protagonist. Your spotlight may be on a fictional protagonist when you realize they are identifying with the story in a way you think is inappropriate in that moment. Your responsibility is to safely allow them, or ask them, to let someone else play. Unless you are trained to do so, this work is not about group therapy through role play. That is a different use for this type of theatre process. This work is group problem solving, exploration, and dialogue.

However, that said, we need only return to Robert Alexander's quote to recall that the act of creating is, in itself, a healthy act, a form of finding one's voice and seeing the world in new ways. In that sense, art is therapeutic. So is this process.

Allow there to sometimes be loose ends. Keep it safe but not always "comfortable." Use your own common sense to watch out for your group but don't be overprotective. Don't be afraid of experience in the process. Be aware of boundaries. Trust your judgment and the work to allow participants to set their own limits. Be there when necessary to reinforce and support those limits.

Improvisation

The activating scene work is based on improvisation work. This section details concepts and activities you can work on with a group to build the skills necessary to engage in improvisational work that goes beyond "role plays." In a single-session arc, these activities can fit into the bridge work, precede the bridge work, or follow the bridge work as steps toward the activating material. In the longer arc of a group process, these activities allow you to go deeper in scene work and should be returned to often. The imagination is a muscle, and playing improv (from here on, short for *improvisation*) games keeps that muscle strong, creative, and able to make specific, human choices that will pay off as you explore decision making and realistic human behavior. You can't improvise enough. A group is never done learning about these skills or about themselves.

Why This Work Is Different Than Other Theatre

Or, Why It's Often Easier to Work with People Other Than "Theatre People"

Interactive theatre, conceptually, is different than what most people commonly think of as "theatre." Its goals are different, and really, the entire event is different from traditional theatre. Therefore, although skills around performing and creating drama and stage-craft are often transferable to this kind of work, what makes good "theatre" and what makes strong interactive theatre is entirely different. The danger is for people (adults and youths alike) to assume that because they have a background in theatre they will be able to assist teachers or groups with interactive theatre from their present skill level.

This is almost always a recipe for disaster. Anyone with previous theatre experience who becomes a part of this work must be completely willing to reexamine how they view theatre and LEARN NEW THINGS! If they assume they'll come in and share some tips or straighten out some ideas and they have no grounding in these techniques or approaches, they will frustrate you, you will frustrate them, and you will be set off track. When I began working with high schools around the country and many of my projects involved setting up peer education interactive theatre groups, schools would assume I only wanted kids from drama classes. I soon learned to say "I would love to have kids from drama classes, but I would rather take ten kids interested in the issues we are tackling than ten kids who are coming just because they love to act any day—and, we'll have a stronger group."

This work is for anyone willing to work in new ways, learn from the process, learn from others, and learn about themselves.

What Is Improvisation?

I always start work on improv by asking the group that very question. I make it clear that I'm not looking for a right answer but for their preconceptions. I want to know what they think of when they hear the word, and then I explain my definition in terms of how it relates to the work we're doing. If the following words don't come up, I throw them out: *listening, focus, character, pretend, honest,* "in the moment," and *teamwork,* before I give my definition.

I then start with the largest and most common misperception about improv: that it's comedy. So I divide improv into two forms: comedy improv and pure improv. Both valid. Both wonderful—but different. Comedy improv is about getting laughs. It's clever, it's ad-libbing, and it's jokes. It often acknowledges the audience with a wink, letting them know that they're all in on the joke. This kind of improv will go anywhere for a laugh; if someone walks into a scene and says "Mom!" the other person might say "I don't know where you left your glasses, but I'm a fifty-six-year-old man." Denial is one form of sharp contrasting realities and often produces that big laugh.

In pure improv, however, there is no denial. If someone calls you Mom, you are. It is about building together, not tearing down. The common phrase is "Yes, and. . . ." Someone brings a fact into the scene and the other person says, "Yes, and" adding on the next layer, never taking away. *Pure improv involves living in a pretend world, in a given circumstance, from a character's point of view, and playing every moment truthfully and imaginatively.* Truthfully in a pretend world? Sounds confusing, but it's not. Everything about the situation and the environment is fiction, but your action in every moment is dictated not by a need to entertain, but by your own honest human response. That response is filtered through your imagination's vision of the character's point of view whom you are playing. Hope Is Vital is based in pure improv.

These pieces are the foundations of creating structured improvisations that allow you to deal with issues and activating scenes:

location/activity

relationship

circumstance

intention

high stakes

strong, detailed choices.

The following activities address these pieces individually and in groups.

The Feedback Questions

The four questions that you will ask participants to deal with after every pair improv activity are:

1. Did you stay in it?
2. Did you make it important to you?
3. Did you make strong choices and build the story together?
4. What could we have done differently to make the stakes higher?

These four questions are the structure for feedback. Throughout this section on improv I will often say "Have the pairs deal with the feedback questions now." All pairs in the room should have a minute or two to process these questions in relation to the scene/activity they just did. This is an important part of their becoming stronger improvisers and of their working together as an ensemble. They help each other grow through honest critique, observation, and support. They can't just say "You did great" or "We blew it that time." They have to give specific comments on what they did, what worked, what didn't work, and why. As you read on in this section and get a clearer idea of the concepts, you will be able to help them with appropriate and constructive feedback ideas.

Activity/Urgency

Number of People: 6 or more
Age Level: All ages
Time: 10–25 minutes
Source: Original via Spolin

The Basic Idea

Everyone gets a partner, and they decide who "A" will be and who "B" will be. "A" has to come up with a physical activity that would be difficult to accomplish alone in four minutes (fixing a flat tire alone, cooking dinner for ten alone, painting a house alone). "B" watches "A" attempt to complete this activity for the first two minutes. Then you shout "B, go," and "B" then dives in and tries to help "A" finish the task in the last two minutes but without either of them talking. So "B" has tried to figure out what's going on while watching during those first two minutes. One more note for "A": they must have a *reason why* the activity has to be done in four minutes. It's not good enough to rush because "it's important." Why is it important? "A" must have a specific reason for needing to finish and specific consequences that will occur if the activity is not finished. After the four minutes are up, you yell "freeze" and make sure they don't talk to each other right away. Go around the space and have each "B" say what they think they were doing and then each "A" say what they were actually doing. Also, have "A" give the reason for needing to complete the activity; push "A" to be specific and to make up details right then if he or she needs to. Then have "A" and "B" switch roles and do it again.

> *Silence is important in this and other activities because it demands that participants relate to each other physically and spatially, as well as relate to the environment around them instead of filling the environment with random talk. Silence insists on a form of communication that speech often doesn't convey.*

Reminders

- As in all improv games remind them to focus and stay in the scene with their partner. They should not be distracted by the other pairs.

- Remind them throughout to make the task important to them (especially "A" in the first round). How important they make this task determines how involved they will both get in accomplishing it. This has everything to do with their specific reasons for needing it done in four minutes.
- This is a silent game.
- Make sure "A" picks an activity that is physical and specific (putting groceries away as opposed to carrying bags inside, or baking a cake as opposed to buying a cake).

Thoughts

This game introduces the idea of two people working and playing together, trying to achieve a common goal, and doing these under time and circumstance constraints. It's a great exercise in creating high stakes—that energy that motivates us often in life and we try to re-create in improv work with specific, imaginative choices and a gut-level belief in the pretend moment. You can also play this game with small groups, either by giving them or having them come up with activities and time urgencies, and then having others join in.

Relationships

The way we act in life has to do with the relationships we have with the people around us. You act differently around your mother, say, than you do with a friend, and differently with your teacher than either of them. We all play roles. I'm not talking about behaving phony. I'm talking about the way our behavior shifts depending on the relationship you have with a person in any given situation. One of the most important guideposts for establishing what is going on and how one should respond in an improvised scene is to determine the relationship between the characters involved. This can be determined before and/or during the scene depending on the activity and the goals in that instant of work. The questions to ask when playing relationships are, What are the qualities of specific relationships that are universal, and what are the qualities that are cliché and stereotypical? How do you make relationships real, detailed, and unique?

For starters, as with all improv work, by practicing.

Relationship Wheel

Number of People: 8 or more
Age Level: All ages
Time: 20–40 minutes
Source: Original

The Basic Idea

Everyone gets a partner, and the pairs all make a big circle around you. (This requires some space.) The partners decide who "A" will be and who "B" will be. You will call out a relationship and an activity (for example, doctor/patient: examination). They will each silently begin to engage in that activity as characters in that relationship. They can't talk about who is which, they just start. After a minute or two, you say "speech," at which point they continue not only with the relationship and the activity but begin speaking. The dialogue comes right out of whatever moment the scene had progressed to silently. They pick up the situation in midaction. They don't start over. After a couple of minutes in speech mode you say "freeze, switch." All the "A" partners shift one person to the right so that everyone has a new partner. Without allowing any conversation you quickly call out a new relationship and activity. So the order of your calls is like this:

"Relationship: doctor/patient; Activity: examination. Silently, go!"

1–2 minutes pass

"Speech."

2–3 minutes pass

"Freeze. Don't talk. Switch. Silently!"

"A"s rotate one person to the right.

"Relationship: parent/child; Activity: packing. Silently, go!"

and so on.

Other relationships and activities suggestions:

> Siblings; cooking
>
> Teacher/student; searching
>
> Teammates; warming up
>
> Ex-lovers; shopping
>
> Good friends; spying

You can come up with more on your own or with your group.

Reminders

- Remind them not to be distracted by the other pairs. This is an activity that demands concentration and decreases self-consciousness because everyone is playing at once.
- When silent, they should not be mouthing words. Fake talking is a *terrible,* TERRIBLE habit for actors. It means nothing, and it prevents you from actually being involved in what could be going on. Keep your focus on the activity and the quality of the relationship.
- When I say "quality of the relationship," I'm referring to the tone of the interaction between the two people. How they relate. Is it comfortable, loving, based on power or authority, nervous, nasty? This quality will directly determine what is said and how it is said once speech begins. The speaking scene does not come out of a vacuum. It comes from what has been created through the activity within the relationship during the silent part of the game.

Thoughts

This exercise demands that participants listen to each other, which is a lesson both for improvisation and for this whole process. Here you will get a sense of where their focus is and how comfortable they are with jumping into scenes. When you process this activity, talk about challenges and things people found easy while playing. Ask if they got stuck or if they ran out of ideas. Why do they think that happened? Look for issues and themes of difficulty that different pairs experienced. Did they play as themselves or did they find characters? Were all of their scenes arguments or were they able to be there without conflict? Which of those two things is easier, and why? These things will start to make even more sense as you add the next piece: intention.

Intention

What does one person in a scene want from another person? What do they need? That is an *intention*. Intention is the driving force that propels a character in a given situation to take action and move through a scene *with a reason* to accomplish something. It drives them to get what they want and what they need. The strength, clarity, and importance of a character's choice of intention determines the behavior and course of a character in a specific interaction. This includes the strategies and tactics the character uses to get what they want.

Drama comes from conflicting intentions. If I want something and you want something else, we are in conflict. You won't let me have what I need and I won't give you what you need. Two people playing "yes/no," caught in a stalemate of not budging, is boring. Two human beings, each struggling to get what they need from someone who is important to them, is dramatic. Characters building a story with detail, and specific moments that raise the stakes and deepen the connection between them, is engaging. The next couple of exercises deal with that.

Russel's Soup (A/B)

Number of People: 6 or more
Age Level: All ages
Time: 15–40 minutes
Source: Original

The Basic Idea

Everyone gets a partner, and they decide who "A" will be and who "B" will be. "A" starts a physical activity (cooking, fishing, cleaning, performing surgery) and "B" watches. While "B" watches, they have to come up with the relationship that "A" and "B" will have to each other. "B" decides without telling "A." "B" also comes up with a strong intention, something important that they want from "A" in the context of the relationship they have chosen. When "B" has quickly figured out these two things, they enter the space. All the pairs are going at once, and the "B" partner enters at their own pace. Once "B" enters, the scene starts. They should not walk in and say "Hi, Mom." The idea is for the relationship to become clear from the way (behavior, dialogue, and tone) "B" interacts with "A."

> *This game is soup because, when played well, it mixes together all the key improv pieces: relationship, intention, location, activity, high stakes, strong detailed choices, and circumstance. Play it again and again and again . . .*

"A" tries to figure out the relationship while continuing to focus on the activity and playing the scene, slightly in the dark. The key is listening and adapting to what each person brings to the scene. As "A" is trying to figure out the relationship, "B" is beginning to try to get their intention. As "A" begins to realize what "B" wants, it is "A"'s responsibility to make choices that allow them, as a character, to not give in. "A" needs to come up with details as the two create a story together, and to want something from "B" in opposition to what "B" wants. The conflict builds, the story grows, and the relationship deepens. The scene does not resolve—it goes on as the energy in the room rises until you shout "freeze." Then, each pair spends a minute or two on the feedback questions. After that, with the same partner they go again. This time "A" and "B" switch tasks and it's a brand-new scene.

After I explain this the first time I always get a volunteer and play a sample round in front of the group so they can get an idea of what it looks like. Here's an example of how a scene might look:

> Jessica starts in the space and is serving soda to customers. I come in and it soon becomes clear we're teenage friends (that's the relationship I chose) at a carnival in a small town where we live and where she's working. I make small talk (you don't want to just blurt your intention out) and I get around to asking if she'll help me "borrow" one of her dad's guns later tonight (the intention I chose). She wants to know why (she's still busy serving soda as this is discreetly being talked about) and I beat around the bush. Finally, she says she won't even talk about it further if I don't say why. So I tell her I've been having some trouble with some guys and that some friends and I are going to meet them later tonight and my friends think we should have a gun just to make a strong showing. She gets very upset and she (Jessica, the actress) makes the very strong choice that her brother was killed a couple of years ago in gun violence and she'll be damned if she'll lose someone else she cares about. The conversation turns into an emotional confrontation about friendship, fear, and peer pressure. I tell her I'm afraid for my life and she says we can talk to her dad, at which point I say there's no way I'm talking to the sheriff about this (a strong choice on my part, to make her dad the sheriff in that moment). It ends with me saying "freeze" after I give her an ultimatum: help me get a gun or lose a friendship. We stop and talk with the group about the four feedback questions (especially about strong choices we made). These strong choices were detailed choices and helped build the conflict as we built the story together. The group was a little intimidated because it was such an intense first scene but I remind them that all scenes don't have to be life and death. They do need to be important and interesting enough for them to maintain a five- to fifteen-minute scene.

Reminders
- They should pick relationships that can have high stakes. In other words, losing the relationship would matter. Strangers usually don't have anything at stake in a conflict because when they go their separate ways, that's it. People who are in each

other's lives have to deal with repercussions. The stakes are higher.

- Pick strong intentions. "I want you to feed my goldfish" is not strong or interesting. "I want you to take my large, drooling dog for two months while I travel" is strong and could be interesting.

- Remember: "I want to tell you something" is *not* an intention. "I want you to keep a secret" *is*. "I want to apologize" is *not* an intention. "I want you to accept my apology" *is*. It must be something you want from the other person. It must be specific, clear, active, and strong.

- Remind them to try to keep their scenes standing or moving. Sitting scenes can become conversational, inactive, and casual. Avoid CASUAL!

- If they ever get stuck in a scene and aren't sure where to go next, remind them that they don't have to always be talking. Silence is fine. Most important, when they get lost they should go back to the activity. They will find ideas and flow in the pretend environment and their activity is the key to that. Tell them to let it ground them in the world they've created and the next moment will surprise them by simply happening.

Thoughts

You want them to start creating stories together in these scenes. The choices they make while listening to each other and building details into histories and connections are incredibly important. These choices and details are the difference between role plays and theatre. Human beings we care about versus the generic, nonspecific "boyfriend/girlfriend" debate that so often passes for scene work in a classroom. You are working on the group's ability to involve their bodies, voices, minds, hearts, and souls in these pretend encounters, these fictions. These foundation pieces (activity, relationship, intention, and so on) are the framework in which to practice.

Line Improvs

Number of People: 6 or more (you need space)
Age Level: All ages (find age-appropriate scenarios)
Time: 10–30 minutes
Source: Original via Living Stage

The Basic Idea

Everyone breaks into two even-numbered single-file lines facing each other. The lines back away from each other (about 10 paces), and each person should know who is directly across from them: their partner. You explain that in Russel's Soup they had to make all the initial decisions and build from there. In this game you will provide them with the relationship, the circumstance, and the intentions. Their responsibility will be to build the conflict and the story together; make strong, detailed choices; and allow the stakes to be high. Here is an example so the mechanics of the game are clear in a specific context:

The relationship is parent/child. One line is "Parent," the other is "Child." The child has to be fourteen to nineteen years old. The child wants to go to a rally, demonstration, or protest going on in the community tonight. The cause behind the gathering is important to them, and they are coming to ask for permission to attend. The parent does not want them to go at all. Not at all.

The details, the kind of rally, the reasons for not letting them go are choices to be made by the players. When you say "go," the "Child" line crosses the space at once and walks up to their "Parent." The scene takes place face-to-face—no moving around, no sitting— standing there, confrontation style. After five to fifteen minutes, call out "freeze," and have them respond to the four feedback questions in their pairs. Then start over by having one line rotate so that everyone is looking across at a new person. Have these new pairs go ahead with a new scenario.

Reminders

- They should, at this point, be challenging themselves to take on points of view that are different from their own. So, the rally should not be a cause they are personally passionate about but rather something they have to work at to be passionate about. They should be playing characters that are uncomfortable for them (this is specifically addressed in an upcoming section) and not just another version of their own worldview.

- Focus on details. The story should grow richer and deeper from the moment they start until you shout "freeze."
- They are not looking for resolution. They are building conflict. This will make more sense when you begin to work on activating material.
- Some decisions they can make in the 15 seconds you give them before you shout "go." Others they can't make until the scene starts.

Examples of Other Line Improv Setups

Good friends. The one who will remain in place has been dating someone for six months and they haven't gotten much support from anyone regarding the relationship. Today, for the first time, the friend who is crossing the space says they want their friend to break up with the person they're seeing because of the group the person they're dating is part of (this could be about race, religion, socio-economic status, gender).

Siblings. Both go to the same high school. The one crossing is approaching their sibling because they believe they have a substance abuse problem. They want them to get help today from the school counselor or they'll tell their parents. The accused doesn't think they have a problem.

Lovers. The one approaching has heard that a former partner of their current partner (here) is rumored to be HIV+. They want the two of them to go get tested together. The approached feels there is no way they could be positive and doesn't want to go.

Note that each one has a clear relationship, circumstance, intention, and conflict. Set these things up and create your own line improvs. They don't have to relate specifically to issues.

Thoughts

This is a powerful exercise that raises the intensity level in the room. You want to feel that a group is ready for it, trustwise and skillwise. However, there is also something to be said for diving in and processing the experience. You learn from wherever you're at, and you don't want to be overly cautious. If the conflicts don't build as the round goes on, or if they peak early and people are left with nothing to really go with before the end, make sure you talk about that. The four feedback questions are always a great starting point, as well as discussing the current state of comfort in the group, in the space. A group needs to be able to play this game with energy and focus before they are truly ready to move into engaging, activating material.

Going to Uncomfortable Places

In the note on tension and laughter, I mentioned that our instinctual response to tension is to try to release it. Similarly, when in an improvisational scene that requires us to be in an uncomfortable situation (within the fiction of the scene or because of the contrast between our own views and our character's views), we want to respond as we do in uncomfortable situations in real life: We want to get out. In improv work, we are practicing to stay in those pretend situations so we can examine them and learn from them.

This is complicated by the fact that when we are in an imaginary situation, if we truly allow ourselves to experience the imaginary circumstance and everything else going on, our body has a real reaction. Our body has a chemical, physiological response that is no different from real life. I'm not saying that in that moment we don't know that it's pretend. We do, but our body releases adrenaline and pumps our heart up and whatever else it does for that perceived emotional instant. That can be scary. It can also be exhilarating. The way to get used to that is by doing it and by talking about it, making sure that everyone in the space feels comfortable enough to acknowledge any discomfort in any moment and step out. Encourage them to push themselves but remind them that they can and should take responsibility for their own well-being. Let your common sense and the process once again be your guide.

Exit

Number of People: 6 or more
Age Level: All ages
Time: 10–20 minutes
Source: Original

The Basic Idea

Everyone gets a partner and decides who "A" is and who "B" is. This is a simple, quick game that demands immediate, strong choices. You say "You are inside some space together. 'A,' you want to leave. 'B,' you want them to stay. Go!" They immediately play the scene for 3–5 minutes. They freeze, and they discuss the four feedback questions with their partner. Then, they switch roles and do it again in a new scene.

Reminders

- They should have quickly established relationship, circumstance, and filled in their intentions with details. Check with them after the first round to see if they built stories or if they got stuck.
- You can get a sense by watching them here if they're using their bodies in the space to get involved in activities and use the environment to their advantage, or if they're talking and standing, not physically engaged. Give them group feedback on that.

Thoughts

The fun here is taking a blank slate and bringing it to life. The final games in this section are still about skill building, but they're really about taking joy in creating stories and finding the particulars of human interaction. The excitement is in not knowing what comes next and working so well with other people that fear is replaced with an energizing calmness. This joy is necessary and intrinsic to bring characters to full life as you begin to use them to explore issues and decision making. It is work, and it should also, most definitely, be play.

Entrance

Number of People: 6 or more
Age Level: All ages
Time: 10–20 minutes
Source: Original

The Basic Idea
It's like Exit, but in reverse. Everyone gets a partner and they decide who "A" is and who "B" is. You say "'A,' you are in a space. 'B,' you want to come in. 'A,' you don't want them to. Go!" They play for 3–5 minutes. They freeze and discuss the feedback questions. They reverse roles and they do it again.

Reminders
• The same as in Exit. Come up with specific details creating stories and connections, strong choices, and enjoy the play.

Thoughts
As you find other improv games from other sources to keep things fresh, also realize that you can create your own games. Sometimes combining two games you know can result in a great twist. For instance, play Exit, then after they've processed, tell them the game is Entrance, it's the next day and they're the same characters from the round of Exit they just played. The person who threw out the other person in Exit now wants to get in somewhere the next day! How can they make that make sense? What emotionally has to happen? What curves does the story take? You can talk about those things after the round. What other ways can you create new games as you go on? Make yourself be creative. Don't just count on what other sources give you. Challenge yourself.

Image Alive

Number of People: 6 or more
Age Level: All ages
Time: 15–40 minutes
Source: Original via Boal

The Basic Idea

This game comes directly out of the bridge activity Complete the Image. If you remember it in detail, continue reading. If not, you may want to go back and remind yourself how it's played. You have pairs spread out around the room playing Complete the Image and after a couple of minutes you shout "freeze, image alive!" At that moment, the pairs start a scene from the position they are frozen in. They can move, but the initial activity, the relationship, and the dialogue need to start from that frozen position. They will establish a relationship but, beyond that, you will have told them ahead of time what the goals are. Some possible ones include:

Should they find intentions and a circumstance and build conflict?

Should they only play the relationship and just see where it goes?

Should they play a scene that stems from a theme you have given them?

The scenes go on for only a couple of minutes and then you say "freeze, back to Complete the Image. Silently. Go!" After another minute or two, "freeze, image alive!," and so on. Each time it's a brand-new scene. When you stop the game you can have them process the feedback questions in pairs and then process the whole activity as a group. A good question to ask everyone is What did you learn about what you need to work on specifically as an improviser? This is a great game to return to often.

Reminders

• When you shout "freeze, image alive!," a good hint to help them use their position to launch the scene is to reach into the space immediately for an imaginary object or activity instead of retreating physically and searching for a first line. Reach in and let the physicality activate your imagination. Things will flow from there.

- Again: details, strong choices, and specifics. Keep harping on these things.
- Don't let them pause before starting scenes or moving back to Complete the Image. It should all be fluid, not filled with thinking and planning.

Thoughts

This game is another great way to bring two parts of the process together. It creates a sense of purpose and forward motion, and works to help a group see connections. As an improv activity, it's challenging. When a group can fly with these very open-ended games you'll see the resulting depth and energy spill over into activating scene work.

Line/Location/Theme

Number of People: 6 or more
Age Level: All ages
Time: 10–40 minutes
Source: Original via Spolin

The Basic Idea

Everyone sits on the floor and faces the largest open space in the room. Four to six people volunteer and make a single-file line facing the rest of the group. The first person enters the playing space and starts a pretend physical activity. The second person enters after a couple of seconds and begins a scene. In a minute or two they try to create specific characters, a relationship, and they begin to let a story and history appear. Then, you call out "freeze" and the first person goes to the back of the line. The second person freezes for a moment, then starts a new physical activity, and a third person comes in and starts a new scene and so on. You can go through the line as many times as you choose. By keeping it quick, each person has to make instant, strong choices; plus, they have to listen and truly work together.

You also get to choose a focus. All the scenes could take place in the same location. All the scenes could be tied to a theme (jealousy, romance, alcohol). You could go through the line twice and have the characters reoccur so the story can build on interaction and facts brought up in other scenes, or it can be an entirely "clean slate" with no connecting idea or theme. They simply create detailed stories as they play together. After each round, talk with the group about the four feedback questions in relation to the scenes they just saw. This is an activity that really has them up performing in front of each other. Ask: How did that feel?

Reminders

- This is not the popular comedy-improv game Freeze Tag. That game is quicker and is all about one-liners and gags and it doesn't lead to developing relationships and circumstances. The goal here isn't to entertain but to play the truth of the pretend moment.

• Remind them to allow the activity to be an integral part of the scene and to help them make discoveries about the situation.

Thoughts

This is a good opportunity to take the skills and focus they've been working on and observe how an audience affects them. Do they continue to play moments truthfully or do they play for laughs? That will certainly happen some and you can talk about why and how to concentrate through it. It helps to focus on the other person, on the activity, and on what you want in the scene. Also, *focus on making the imaginary world and imaginary circumstance real and important.* Pretend with all your might. And enjoy.

Thoughts on Continuing Improv Work

No one is ever done learning how to improvise. The more you play, the better you get; but the truly odd part is if you don't keep playing, you don't stay at the same level. You get worse. You get stale. Your work becomes dull and limited. You always have to return to these games (or others you bring in) throughout your process, whether that time period is long or short.

A common refrain from a group at some point might be "We've played that game" or "We've done enough improv" or "That game gets boring." These are learning moments. They are times when the most interesting improv work is soon to come because, you see, improv games are just structures. What happens in them, what the participants actually get to play, is totally up to them. Up to them! *They* create the stories. *They* create the characters. *They* create the conflict. The games are never the same twice. If they are bored, they are boring themselves and it's their responsibility to make the scenes interesting for themselves. Don't feel a need to entertain them through all of these moments. Challenge the group to find new ideas. Throw out some ideas if you like but put the burden on them. Once you start, don't let nonissue, fun, skill building improv games be away from your work for too long.

Activating Material

Not a Role Play, Not Role Modeling, Not a Skit

An activating scene grabs everyone in the room. It is a scene that you create with your group. People need to care about it, recognize it, and be pulled into the drama of it. Most important, people must want to effect change in what they see. They need to see a clear opportunity to get involved and to explore options. An activating scene does not show *what to do*. It does not have a message. It asks *what can be done.*

The Uniqueness of Activating Theatre

In order to clearly lay out the uniqueness of activating theatre, let's generalize the experience most modern theatre (plays) offers an audience. You, the audience, follow a main character through the story. You get involved with a protagonist. You care about him or her. You go on a journey and watch the protagonist deal with trials, tribulations, and triumphs. If it's a good play, as the conflict(s) build(s) around the protagonist, you are pulled forward in your seat, actually pulled toward the stage, as you wait for a resolution you hope will be satisfying. You watch. You wait. You care . . . and choices are made. Action is taken, or not, and the play comes to its conclusion. You are released. You know the ritual. The curtain falls, literally or figuratively, and you share your appreciation for the event with polite applause, and you leave. The story is over, and most of the time (*great* theatre and good Brecht plays aside) your need to think and to take action has been soothed. The experience ends passively and you leave having witnessed others take action for you. Whether it touched you and your desires or not, the course human life took on stage was predetermined. You go on.

In the type of interactive theatre that Hope Is Vital creates, activating scenes are shorter than full-length plays. They are compressed scenarios that relate specifically—either realistically or metaphorically—to the lives of the participants in the room. The scenes pull the audience (of participants) into the story. They bring you forward to the edge of your seat, and they freeze. They end, or stop, unsatisfactorily. You, the audience, are left with a strong desire—a *need*—to change what is happening, and you get that chance. As soon as the scene stops, the facilitator, who was responsible for stopping the scene by calling "freeze" (this role will be expanded on later), turns to you and says "Is this real?" Through the process of questioning, the facilitator quickly gets some of you up into the story. They give you an opportunity to explore what is going on and an opportunity to effect change. You are given an opportunity to *replace* the protagonist and discover options.

But the focus of replacement in this scene is clearly on one character, because you and your group have created a scene with a protagonist who is clearly trying to accomplish something and failing. It is the protagonist's believable failure and the audience's desire for him or her to succeed that inspires the dialogue within this activation and facilitation process. I'll use the following activating scene to relate the mechanics of activating material.

An Activating Scene

This scene was created in a town of 15,000 in Oregon and done for the first time at an open community forum held for youths and adults in that community. Sixty people came, and I facilitated. The youths in the group identified sexual harassment as an issue with which they wanted to deal. They posed two questions they wanted the scene to address. As you read the description of the scene see if you can pinpoint what those two questions were.

Note: I've compressed the scene and dialogue here, because it was almost 8–10 minutes long.

The scene starts with a sixteen-year-old girl standing alone in the space, bouncing an imaginary volleyball. It turns out she's in the school gym. She has recently moved to this town from a smaller, more rural town where she was a volleyball star. She's arrived at school in October, when the school year has already started. The volleyball team has started practices, so she's here after school at 5:00 P.M. on a Monday to meet with the volleyball coach, a thirty-five-year-old man. He's agreed to see her play and decide if she can join the squad or if she has to play junior varsity. Being new in town, we soon realize making varsity is important to her because it will help her enter her new environment with a certain level of status that she wouldn't have otherwise. We discover this early in the scene in the conversation between the two, not from a pre-scene narration.

The coach enters and asks her to serve a couple of balls. She does and he moves around her, watching her intently. He asks her to take her initial position as she is preparing to serve. She does, and he comes over to her, correcting her position with a hand on her knee and the other hand on her lower back. She serves some more and then he asks her to show him some sets. She does and he shouts "freeze" as she's in an outstretched position. She freezes and he comes over to her, correcting her position again, one hand a little above the knee and the other a little lower on her back than before. She appears a tiny bit uncomfortable. She sets some more and then he tells her to stop. He says that she's got definite potential and that he's willing to work with her.

She says, "So, I'm on the team?"

He says, "No, but I think you can be. You need to work some

more with me first. You and I will work out after practice every day from five to 6:30 P.M. for the next two weeks, and if I think you've made enough progress, you'll join the squad after that."

She's confused. "You mean we'll work alone?"

"That's right. I'll give you extra instruction and we'll see how you do."

There is a pause.

"Couldn't I just join the team and you could work with me there?"

He starts to get frustrated. "Do you understand the opportunity I'm offering you? Do you know how many players here would like extra attention, extra time with me? You said you were a varsity-level player."

"I am."

"So where is your commitment? Where's your dedication? Let me see you serve again."

She does. He calls out "freeze." He goes to her and, as he corrects her positioning, says, "You show promise. You've got to be willing to work."

She says, "All right. I'll talk to my parents about it and I'll come find you tomorrow."

"We start now."

"Today?"

"Yes, today."

"But, my parents are expecting me home soon. I've got home-work to do. I can't stay today."

He blows up in a coach, locker-room-talk kind of way. "Why are you wasting my time. Why are you even here? I have a cham-pionship-level team. I am offering you the opportunity to play for that kind of team, and all you do is give me excuses. Where is your dedication? Show me some dedication. If you want to play for this team you will go to the phone right now, call your parents, and tell them that practice is going late today. You'll be home for a late supper. If you don't want to do that, fine. You can play junior varsity. I have more important things to do with my time than wait for a new student to figure out her priorities."

There is a pause.

He says, "Now, what's it going to be?"

Another pause.

She says, "I'll, um, I'll go call my folks, and, uh, I guess I'll be right back. I'll be right back."

She walks off and he stands alone bouncing the ball.

I, as the facilitator, shout "freeze." The audience is all leaning forward, intensely involved, frustrated, mad, upset, and not satisfied with the turn of events.

I ask them if the scene was realistic. An overwhelming "yes" is the response. After a couple other questions about what went on, including diverse opinions on whether or not "harassment" took place, I ask what the girl wanted. There are a variety of responses, mostly along the lines of "to be treated respectfully"; "to not be harassed"; "to have an honest shot at being on the team"; "to have him recognize the inappropriateness of his behavior." I ask if she got what she wanted, and get an overwhelming response of "no." I ask if there were other things she could have done to try and get what she wanted. "Yes" responses ripple through the group. I ask "like what?" Hands go up. We're off. I begin to bring people up and replace the protagonist to explore the options available to her in the minds and gut of this community, here represented by sixty young people and adults. But, it is more complex than replacing her over and over again, so I'm going to leave off how this process developed here for a time. I want to briefly look at why this scene is a successful activating scene; then, in the next section on facilitation, I'm going to come back to this instant in the process and continue to examine facilitation using this example.

The Difference Between an Activating Scene and a Message Scene

The scene above offers an opportunity to delineate between a modeling scene and an activating scene and shows how much more actual education takes place through the facilitation process.

If this scene were done in the standard style of message plays, here is what would occur: As the coach began to be inappropriate (in the eyes of whoever created the scene), the girl, deciding she was uncomfortable, would confront him and perhaps say, "Hey! You can't treat me like that, that's inappropriate, and I'm going right now to talk to the principal, the school board, and my parents. You're done here, mister!"

The audience would cheer, and there would be a good feeling all around. The message would be clear: young women do not have to put up with that type of treatment and have every right to respond as the young woman in the scene did. Thank you and good luck. Like in the previous example of "theatre," the audience's need to take action, to consider and to problem solve, is gone. *The solution has been presented, and dialogue is not only absent, it's unnecessary.*

No one would argue that the message is a good one. It's important to let young women know that they should not tolerate being treated in that manner. But in terms of prevention, education, and dialogue, the message scene is completely ineffective. However, the activating scene, rather than soothe the audience with a satisfying resolution, *demands* the audience's help in figuring out WHAT TO DO! Because the power of theatre has involved them emotionally in the situation, they care about the outcome, and they are left with a need to struggle with possibilities.

Checklist for an Activating Scene

These are the specific things that made this scene activating:

❏ A believable and realistic situation
❏ A previously structured but not scripted scene (it was reimprovised to feel spontaneous and real, and strong improv skills allowed this to happen successfully)
❏ The scene revolved around a moment of decision—Would she stay or go?—and her decision left us *wanting something different*
❏ It has a clear relationship, intentions, circumstance, location, activity, high stakes, and two people listening to each other and connecting in the pretend moment
❏ A conflict that is clear
❏ A protagonist that the audience cared about and with whom they could identify
❏ An antagonist(s) or "villain(s)" that wasn't evil and cartoony

but was credible, strong, and had certain ambiguities around his actions that made him human (he was not groping her like crazy and he never spoke of sex at all; he was subtle)

❏ A clear idea of what the protagonist wanted and didn't want

❏ The protagonist's failure to get what she wanted

❏ The reason for failure clearly being the strong actions, attitudes, and choices of the antagonist(s)

❏ A clear sense that the protagonist had inner voices, or desires, that reinforced her inability to succeed (this sixteen-year-old was new at school, wanted varsity status socially, and being from a small town, felt she had to prove herself)

This checklist can help you put together activating scenes. Every piece is important. *A clear protagonist in a moment of decision failing to get what they want* forces you to focus ahead of time on who you want to replace and what the decision you're exploring is. The idea is not to manipulate the group into saying what is right and wrong but to look at the issue at hand from the perspective of characters who want to make certain choices but are unable to carry them out. This then allows you to investigate the reality, the wisdom, and the potential of those choices within real-life circumstances, and actively analyze strategies and possibilities with everyone in the room through the replacement process. In the facilitation section, I look in more detail at how facilitating opens up a scene and a dialogue to carry out this exploration.

Activating Scenes Pose Questions

Before I described the scene, I asked you to try to figure out what two questions it was trying to address. This work is about *posing* questions, not providing but *exploring answers or options*. Questions are often a better place to start when creating activating scenes than just general topics. Questions give you a focus and direction. The scene here is about sexual harassment, but more specifically, it asks:

What is sexual harassment?
and
What can someone do when they feel they are being sexually harassed?

Both questions are asked. The second is clearly dealt with when people replace the girl and try to deal with the situation. The first is dealt with through the dialogue the facilitator leads as (s)he prods the audience into a discussion about what they feel is going on here. The facilitator deals with the strong emotional response to support the protagonist but also with the issue as it exists in the scene. Would different people define harassment differently and how would that impact the protagonist's options? Again, this is part of the facilitation process looked at in the next section.

Methods to Develop Activating Scenes

Creating an activating scene essentially involves creating a story, fleshing it out, and making the scene work using the checklist as a guide. I mentioned that questions help you hone in on the decisions and moments you want to explore. You can also use general topics. It just means more work to get to the heart of the issue at hand. That process, however, can be useful as the variety of meanings a topic holds for different individuals becomes a part of the exploration itself. Here are four ways to work with groups to develop material. I will not elaborate in great detail here because the bottom line is that *you can only truly learn about activation (and facilitation) by doing it.* Here are some starting points.

Monologues
These are described in Bridge Activities (page 68), which you should go back to and read.

After the participant has told their story and the group has interviewed them in character, you could ask the group what possibilities for activating scenes they see in this character. This exercise is a great way to get a group thinking about the dynamics necessary for activating scenes to exist. For instance, say the list was from the question "Why do teens choose to be or to not be sexually active?" and one of the reasons on the Yes list was "partner pressure." A young woman chooses that one and creates a character who had sex for the first time with her boyfriend because he pressured her. Her story is about that first time. So, the first obvious choice is to create an activating scene about that event when he pressured her into it. With the group, you quickly figure out (through asking them) details about the relationship as well as about where they are, what they both want, and other specifics. Then you work on the scene with the intention of replacing her after she gives in. If their relationship is important to both of them, and he is not a nasty, cartoony guy but still pressures hard, and we can tell that she doesn't want to give in but she does because she doesn't see any other choice, we will be activated to want to look for other options for her. The same scene could be tweaked a little and become a scene where he pressures her to have sex without him using a condom. If she had mentioned in her interview that her friends were pressuring her to lose her virginity and that had contributed to her giving in, the group might decide to create a scene about peer pressure.

The key here is once you move into using a monologue to create an activating scene, you can loosen up the specifics from the story and see where ideas lead you. In other words, just because this story wasn't about condoms and sex, if someone has that idea and the group agrees that it could realistically happen that way, go with it. These characters and stories carry the weight of real life because of the process, even though they are fiction. You can shift things around as you search for material and ideas. Similarly, if the story had been told by the guy (if the guy who did the pressuring was the one who took "partner pressure" from the list and he told this story from his point of view), you could still work the scene with the girl as the protagonist. You could also try a scene where he was pressured by his male friends to have sex with her, and so you make him the protagonist in a scene where he is peer pressured and he gives in. The possibilities are endless. The monologues allow you as a group to meet characters, search for moments of decision in their stories, and imaginatively rummage through the periphery of their story (the rest of their life) while looking for other related ideas for scenes.

Sculpting

Sculpting is described in Bridge Activities on page 62. Feel free to go back and read it.

There are a number of ways you can use sculpting to find activating scenes. Here are some ideas.

- You could split into groups of three or four and do group sculpting (Phase 3 of Sculpting) from a single word like "discrimination." Then have each group pick another group's image and give them one minute alone to talk about what they see in that image. Then tell each group they have to create an activating scene dealing with discrimination using that other group's image as a starting point. Even if the image they saw looked nonrealistic or abstract, they must take the feeling it gave them and develop a scene.

- Again, you could split into groups of three or four. Each participant tells a two- to three-minute true story about a topic such as family and miscommunication. After each story has been told, each group has one minute to create only one image with all members of their group in it that unites the sense of all the threads or themes from their stories and feels complete and representative. They are all clay and they are all sculptors. They can't talk and they must do it in one minute. Then everyone gets to see the other groups' images. Each group, using their own image as a starting point, has to develop an activating scene around the idea of family and miscommunication. It must be fictional, but the image and all the stories inform the topic, the conflict, and the relationships.

  The challenge is sorting through all the ideas your group tosses out and making decisions on your feet. If you spend too much time negotiating which direction the scene should take, the process will lose its forward momentum.

- Form a circle and Circle Sculpt (Phase 4 of Sculpting). Use a topic that the group wants to explore, such as violence. Let the group sculpt for a little while to find a rhythm and go deep with it. When you see an image that strikes you as strong and specific, say "freeze." Then, with the whole group, use that image to quickly develop an activating scene. Ask who the main character is. Ask what is going on. Ask what the relationship is. Ask what each person wants. Perhaps it's an image of two people taunting or threatening a third. Your group may decide that the third person is the protagonist and they are about to be provoked into a fight. The scene is activating because they give in and fight. Your group wants to explore other options for that person in that situation. You need to quickly generate story ideas, and as facilitator, keep a mental checklist of the specifics you need to get from your group to move it to activation. Some peer education groups use this with participants when they go out instead of preparing activating scenes ahead of time. The advantage is you are guaranteed a scene that means something to the people in the room. They created it. The disadvantage is that it's hard to work in this manner at first. It takes practice on the part of the facilitator and on the part of the players who will jump in and improvise the scene immediately, ideally making it activating the first time through. It's a great way to discover what activation really takes, and it's a wonderful way to connect image work directly to the issues.

Machine

Machine is first described in Bridge Activities on page 66 if you'd like to go back and read it through again.

Phase 2 of the Machine description is a human theme machine. The example given there was "alcohol." Let's stick with that. You pick some of the voices the group is drawn to and you can either develop an activating scene all together from one voice or one character, or you can split into small groups and have each group develop an activating scene from different voices. If a voice said "That's enough, OK?" and the person's movement is moving forward, almost reaching out for someone, perhaps the group decides it's a scene about two friends. One is trying to get the other to deal with a drinking problem and the other not only denies the issue completely, but makes the friend feel lousy for even broaching the subject. The protagonist becomes the friend trying to offer support and being rejected. The question is "How do you try to help a friend you think has a substance problem?" Your group then replaces the protagonist and explores options. Like Sculpting, Machine is a great way into the issues through imagination and physicality. Theatre allows entry in ways that straight discussion may not.

Small Groups

Finally, you can simply start with a topic or question and have small groups work on developing activating scenes.

There are a couple of good things that usually happen. It's fascinating to see the different ways groups will tackle an issue, and you get a sense of how clearly the participants have grasped the concept of activation. If all the groups come back with unclear, tepid scenes, you'll know you have more clarifying work to do, not to mention going back to improv work and looking at specifics again.

If the topic is, for example, "disclosure," you can walk around and encourage groups to deal with different facets of that topic. For instance:

- Someone disclosing that they're gay to a person they care about and getting a negative response. Perhaps they become the protagonist as the group looks for ways they can deal with that response and demand respect.
- Someone disclosing to a lover that they've tested positive for HIV and then being abandoned. Perhaps they become the protagonist as the group looks for ways they can get support, not to mention deal with the implications of the partner needing to get tested.
- Someone disclosing to a parent that they're pregnant and getting tossed out of the house. Perhaps they become the protagonist and the group looks for ways they can ask for help and understanding from the parent.

Don't Settle for Role Plays

Out of these different methods for generating activating scenes you will arrive at pieces that sometimes are ready to facilitate and sometimes need more work before they can become activating. It is worth it to put the work and time in to develop these scenes. Although you could facilitate based on the intellectual awareness of what should happen in the scene, if it doesn't actually activate your group, then it's only an exercise in thinking. It's not theatre and it doesn't engage the whole person. The dialogue can go no deeper than a quiet "What if?" or a phony shrillness. Don't settle for role plays. This process has brought you to a place where you can work with your group to find truth and emotion in the situations you have agreed to explore. Therein lies the opportunity to problem solve and have an honest and soulful dialogue.

Troubleshooting to Make Scenes More Activating

Here are some reasons that scenes may not be activating and thoughts and questions to ask yourself on how to work toward that goal after the initial setup.

- Use the checklist shown earlier around the sexual harassment scene and determine if all the necessary pieces are known and in place. This can be very helpful.
- Remember the feedback questions from the improv work. These scenes are improv, so those questions can help you zero in on skills or problems that might be holding you back in regard to a specific scene.
- Is the situation one where the stakes are high for both characters, particularly the protagonist? If not, what can you add or change in the history of the characters, their relationship, or the current circumstance to raise the stakes (for example, a couple that's been together a month versus a couple that's been together six months)? If the stakes are not high, we won't be pulled in.

> *A wonderful, simple way to determine if a scene is activating on the most basic level is to look at the bodies of everyone in the room. If they're not literally pulled toward the scene, if they're relaxed or casual, the scene still needs work.*

- Is the scene not working because the rest of the group simply doesn't buy it? Is it unrealistic in some important aspect (for example, friends blatantly peer pressuring with no clear reason versus friends peer pressuring subtly because their reputations are at stake)? Always ask if it's realistic.
- Is the protagonist unwilling to give in, or do they keep forgetting to give in? This is important and common when you first start working. The actor will not want to appear weak; caught in the emotion of the moment, they will fight back with all their strength. If they say everything there is to say, there will be no need for audience members to come up. Remind them they are sacrificing their strength in the scene for the sake of the dialogue with the audience. They must give in.
- Is the antagonist afraid to pressure too hard or be too mean?

Sometimes, out of a fear of being mean or an uncertainty of how far they can go, the antagonist will not be strong enough for the protagonist to believably give in. Work with the group and the antagonist on realizing that in these fictional worlds it's got to be OK for them to go to extremes. It's necessary for the conflict to build. Much of that conflict is dependent on the credibility of the antagonist's pressure and motivation.

- The scene shouldn't start with the conflict. Like any good improv exercise, it starts with the relationship becoming clear and the details of the story coming out, and then the conflict and the moment of decision begin to appear and build. If the scene is too quick, it's a role play around a topic. If it creates believable characters, relationships, and situations we will care and get involved. Work to allow the scenes to build over some time.

The loud and emotional scene probably felt great to everyone because it was cathartic—it gave everyone in the room an emotional release. Remind them that activating material shouldn't leave them soothed, or released—it should leave them wanting to effect change.

- Shouting and crying are not the same as high stakes and building conflict. Many of the scenes get loud and emotional, but that isn't the goal. The goal is playing the pretend moments honestly. You'll know when it's being done to pump up energy and when the scene is honestly at that pitch. Whispering and soft intensity can be very activating.

- One of the biggest challenges comes when a group presents a dramatic scene that deals with a topic that is very emotional, involves everyone, and there is applause—but it's not activating. It would be great in a play but serves no purpose in an interactive workshop. You have to call that as you see it. You can say, "That was a great scene but it's not activating. There is no opportunity for replacement and no room or need to explore options." It's important that you point out the difference. Just because it made half the room cry and illustrated the issue, it didn't necessarily open it up for dialogue. This will cause some confusion, even consternation at first. You can help by going over what an activating scene is again and possibly taking one of the characters from the scene just done and trying to create an activating scene.

Keeping Your Group Work Safe and Productive

As you work on making scenes more activating with your group, here are two things that will help your working environment feel safe and productive.

1. Do this work all together. Work on the scenes by asking questions and reshaping them through the collective responses filtered through your growing understanding of what it takes to activate a scene. Don't stand up front, go down a checklist, and say what you saw wrong. Work the list together and firmly guide the process. Ask them what worked and what didn't.
2. Make it clear that the feedback on scenes, the critique, and the new directions for performers are not judgment on acting capabilities or on "wrong" ideas. They are to improve character choices and strengthen group work. The whole process is to move the group forward so everyone contributes, gives sometimes, and leads others. Creators don't compete, they collaborate. The collaboration is absolutely part of the dialogue the whole process encompasses.

One last thought before moving on to facilitation: If you are working with a peer education group that will be conducting performance workshops, your practice time is partly about crystallizing these scenes so they're activating and ready. If you are a classroom teacher or working in an ongoing group setting, you may feel that facilitation is the part you truly want to get to. Take some time with setting up the activating scenes so they're strong. As I said above, that time is also a valuable part of the process. It's not wasted. You'll feel the payoff.

Facilitation

Although one could say that leading the whole group theatre process is *facilitating,* when I use the word here I'm specifically referring to the questioning, replacing, and guiding that takes place as a group works through activating scenes. Facilitation is not making a scene activating; we looked at that in the last section. It is actually getting to the meat of this work and playing through the dialogue that results from real activation.

Here is the single most important thing to remember about facilitating: *You get better at it as you do it.* This section offers guiding principles, ideas, tips, tricks, and questions that will help you, but you only get better at it by doing it. Even if you're not sure that you are completely ready, do it. The learning curve jumps tremendously when you stand up there and work with a group. Also, if a scene is really activating, your job as facilitator is much easier, more interesting, and more productive. When a scene is not really activating, you'll have to work harder with lesser results. Finally, when you reach this stage in the process you will realize if your group has known that this is the direction you've been moving in or not. If you have made time throughout the process to talk about this phase and how this is a goal you've been building toward, participants will be ready to jump into scenes. If not, the moment when you open the story to other possibilities may not make sense. Make sure there are no structural surprises. It should be a dialogue the whole way.

What Good Facilitation Looks Like

A good facilitator

- Is energized and enthusiastic about the process. You are the bridge for the participants to move from the audience to the scene. You don't match their energy level because theirs is usually a lower energy at first. You create an environment with its own energy and demand that they come up to it.
- Is a good listener. The group must know you care about their thoughts and their responses and that you are willing to learn as well. This is all signaled by the way you listen: the way you stand, the way you do or don't make eye contact, and the attention you give to their ideas. And, most important, you have to listen to do a good job of knowing where the process can go next.
- Is nonjudgmental. You are not up front to move the scene in the direction you think it should go because of your own opinions. You are working for the participants, completely trusting that these young human beings in a safe, creative environment will naturally explore responsible, healthy directions and possibilities. They will work to take care of each other in the fiction they play in and in the reality of the process you are sharing. To do this you simply must be willing to not judge, to throw away the "lessons" you want to teach, and to allow a dialogue to occur. Be aware of the words you use. Asking if people in the room think the way a character behaved was "wrong" colors the moment. Ask what they think, not if they agree with a certain point of view.
- Deepens the discussion and moves the event forward. Through questioning, you are pushing the group to consider options, angles, and situations in new ways—not by suggesting new things but by sharing observations, looking for consensus, and challenging apathy or surface responses at every opportunity.
- Is confident in your role as tone-setter and guide, not in

having everything all figured out ahead of time. If you are hesitant or nervous it's very hard for others to be comfortable enough to come up into scenes. They need to trust your ability to keep the experience safe. If you are ever unsure as to where to move next, which direction to take a scene, it's very appropriate to ask the group. Clarify where they think the work is going or could go. This is very different than being lost and struggling to retain a sense of control. Be careful when you find your stomach tighten and your instinct telling you to pull in the reins. You are running the process but only in that you are serving the process. If you grab tight for power in a moment of confusion, you will see the dynamic shift and the dialogue stop. It's a delicate balance. Your intention is dialogue and that becomes your authority. Your control is in the fact that everyone in the room knows you are respecting the process you have set up as completely as you are asking them to respect it. Relax, listen, ask questions, and move forward.

- Is aware of the dynamics in the room. Know who is anxious to participate, who is quiet, and who is in the middle. Find ways to involve as many of these different types of people as you can. Work to nudge people, to engage those who often stay disengaged, and to keep a balance by not letting any single person or group dominate.

- Understands that there will be people in the room who don't want to be there. Ideally, you have created a process and event so safe and so much fun, people can't resist participating but some will check out or choose to disrupt. Make it clear that you would love their input at this stage of the process but as with other task-related discipline issues, you need their focus here or the group can't proceed. Don't put them on the spot unless they are truly disruptive. Some people will check out because the issue you're looking at may strike a nerve. Disengagement may be a defense mechanism. Honor that choice. Don't spend too much time on a couple of discipline cases. There is often a feeling that if you send a person out while doing this type of dialogue work you've failed. You didn't let all voices be heard. Not true. Give them an opportunity but don't sacrifice 23 youths who are with you to feel less guilty about one who isn't. Often, if the "checked out" or disruptive person stays around they surprise you and jump in later. They have to earn the right to be involved. There can be no disrespect to others. Stick with that.

- Asks every question truly wanting to hear the answer. Never ask a question, expecting a certain answer with your next move hinging on that response. Often, you may have a good idea of what reaction you'll get at times but you must be prepared for and interested in answers you don't expect. Always move forward from the response you get, not the response you are prepared for or have heard before. Listen.

Steps of Facilitating

Using the sexual harassment scene described in Activating Material as an example, I'm going to go through a standard questioning process. With each scene, the varied specifics may require different questions or unique directions. The following questions, their order, and the paths they can take the scene are clear indicators of a process you can use as a blueprint. I recommend you read the scene description again before continuing.

A couple of other words to describe a good facilitator: provocative, stimulating, patient, and calm.

Although there is no "formula" in this work, these steps are a way to envision breaking down the process:

> Step 1: The Scene
>
> Step 2: The Initial Questioning
>
> Step 3: The First Replacement
>
> Step 4: Processing the Replacement
>
> Step 5: Continuing with Replacements
>
> Step 6: Further Exploration

Step 1: The Scene

The girl walks out, leaving the coach bouncing the ball.
I shout "freeze!"

> *Note well:* While working the scene with the audience, the two actors are loosely frozen in place, in clear view. This allows the audience to suspend their belief and hold on to the tension that the scene has built. The actors can *never* participate in conversations with the group at this point. They can never defend their character choices or clarify what they were trying to do. IT DOESN'T MATTER! All that matters is what the participants saw and how they respond. The actors will release the audience's tension if they come out of character.

Step 2: The Initial Questioning

I turn out and ask:

- *Was the scene realistic?*
  This is always the first question. If more than half say "yes," I go forward. If more than half say "no," I must stop here, listen to them, work with them, and redo the scene so it is realistic to them. Otherwise there's no point. If a minority of participants say it was unrealistic, I'll ask a couple of them why. Even though I will go on, I thank them, telling them since many found it realistic we will continue.

  > *I ask participants to raise their hands with responses. It helps me keep track of the process and it also ensures that responses come to me, which prevents debates happening out in the group.*

- *What was happening? What was going on?*
  Everything moves quickly now and I want as many quick and general responses as I can get. I want to gather their impressions so I know how the scene struck them.
- *Who was the main character?*
  I ask for a show of hands as I point to each actor. In this case, it was the girl, as the group had planned.
- *What did she (the main character) want?*
  This can be one thing or a number of things. Make them be specific. You can use the improv idea of intention as a way to think about it.
- *How did she (the main character) go about trying to get what she wanted?*

You are, with all these questions, looking for brief answers. You don't have to cut people off, but you call on folks quickly, and the energy with which you move things along should make it clear that you are not looking for essays. You also don't have to call on every raised hand for each question.

- *Did she (the main character) get what she wanted?*
  REMEMBER: The scene was activating, so she did not.
  or (depending on the scene)
- *Did she make the decision she wanted to make?*
  This question is one you can come back to later to clarify motivations and search for options if you get stuck.
- *What prevented her from getting what she wanted?*
  or
- *What prevented her from making a choice based on the decision she wanted to make?*
  A quick discussion of the antagonist's role in the conflict and on factors within the protagonist that contributed to her failure, such as her being new in town, wanting varsity status, and so on.
- *What else could she have done to get what she wanted in this situation? What other choices did she have?*
  I allow a quick hearing-out of different ideas, which I am listening to carefully to stockpile suggested strategies for the next step.

> *After every response, I gently echo back to the group what was said. I shorten the response, make sure it is heard, and try to give them all equal weight and time. Some people find it annoying. Some facilitators choose not to do it. I do it through the entire process described here. It works for me.*

Step 3: The First Replacement

I can now go one of two ways. I can ask the person with the third or fourth suggestion to come up and try it, or I can hear out all people with their hands up, pick one that stands out for me, and ask them to come up and try. I nudge, I cajole, and I firmly ask. I get someone to come up to replace the protagonist. Often, it's the first person I ask; sometimes it's difficult to get a first person. Again, it depends on how ready the process has made them. How prepared is the space? This is the final moment where that line between actor and audience is broken. Someone comes up and tries another option. I have everyone applaud for the person coming up and simultaneously acknowledge the person coming out of the scene with the same applause. This appreciation is important and helpful. It keeps the tone supportive.

I ask the participant coming up where they want to start from in the scene. It's up to them. If they say they don't care, I say they have to care, it's now *their* scene. I wait for them to decide. They start and I let them go on until the scene seems to have reached a stopping point *or* (and this is crucial as you move into repeating scenes many times) until I feel all of us watching have a clear idea of what their strategy is. Then, I return to questioning.

Here I must point out two things. Please note: I never turn to the audience and say, "Someone come up and show us what you would do." I stay away from language that personalizes choices. I ask people, "What else could be done?" "What are other possibilities?" This is very important. Although many will be doing what they would like to try themselves, that should remain unsaid. Don't put people on the spot, they won't respond. Or, some might respond but many will shut down. In keeping with that, after the first person completes their intervention, I remind the whole group that as we process and critique what we just saw, we're dealing with a character's choice—not acting ability and not the personal ability of the participant to succeed. The group critique work you did around improv should pay off as you ask the participant who came up to stay out of the discussion of their strategy until the end. Then you can give them a chance to clarify what they were trying to accomplish, and how, as well as what they discovered. You want to watch out for defensiveness, and focus on goals, tactics, and communication.

Step 4: *Processing the First Replacement*

Now, the first participant has come up and taken a shot at the coach. I shout "freeze" and turn to the group to ask:

- *What did this person do differently than the original person?*
  I am asking what her strategy was. What option did she pursue?
- *Did she get what she wanted?*
  Did it work? What did they see happen?
- *Was it realistic?*
  This is an important question at this point. The first person up might have gone to an extreme and behaved in a way that was

not possible for many participants to imagine. They might have confidently rebuked the coach and yelled at him. This provides a great opportunity to discuss what is possible and what is not, reminding everyone that possible is a fluid concept—that is, different for everybody in the room. Hence, the significance of options versus answers or solutions. Nothing presented will work or seem doable for everyone. Some might even find yelling at the coach ludicrous in the given circumstance, but it all opens up ways of seeing the situation. Again, you're keeping the discussion quick and finishing by allowing the person who came in to clarify their intentions and share discoveries. Quickly, also, because the focus is on getting more people into the scene.

So with that first replacement person still standing up there, you then turn out to get another participant up, using any or all of the following questions:

- *Would that option work for everyone?*

- *What are other things she could do in this situation?*

- *What other choices does she have?*

- *Has she gotten what you all said she wanted?*

- *How else could she get any of those things?*

Step 5: Further Replacements

Now several things could happen after the first replacement. Another person might be ready to jump right in or you might have kept good track of ideas offered at the beginning before the first person came up and you simply turn to one of those folks and ask them if they would come and try what they mentioned before. Sometimes the first replacement may have come in so strong and clear that your group feels that they succeeded and there is no need to offer more options. They feel the problem has been solved. It is of the utmost importance, if that moment arises, that you firmly point out the need for a variety of options, a veritable arsenal of tactics. The group has already acknowledged that different approaches will work for different people so you cannot let them stop as if an answer has been found. This often takes quick, skillful requestioning and a simple challenge:

> You have told me that this character did not get what she wanted
> in the original scene. Are you now telling me that what we have
> just witnessed is the only possible way she can, indeed, get what
> she wants? Is this the only way she can stick with the decision
> you said she wants to make? I find that hard to believe. Would
> this option work for everyone? Then what else? What else could
> happen here? What else could she do?

I allow pauses before and after this moment. I feel it's important to
push beyond easy single answers if a group gets stuck. I won't
suggest ideas or strategies, but I will prod.

At this point, you can bring people up, one after another, to
explore the situation and problem solve. How long do you go on
replacing the protagonist? What other directions do you take? How
do you keep the dialogue fresh and alive? The "answers" to these
questions have to do with your goals, your time limitations, and
other factors. To address them, let's examine a few more of the
dynamics that may arise at this point in the process and then close
out this section by sharing Step 6, a couple of techniques that help
deepen the replacement phase.

Issues of Facilitation

Replace the Protagonist

You start by replacing the protagonist. That is your focus. The scene
has been developed to problem solve from the point of view of the
protagonist. A problem some facilitators have is allowing audience
members to come up to replace the antagonist. Someone wants to
see the coach as a nice guy so they come up and the coach is a nice
guy. We see the scene as a fantasy version, an ideal of how we would
like it to appear. After all, the girl did nothing wrong. Why should
she have to change? It's the coach who should change. THAT'S NOT
THE POINT. The group has agreed that the situation is a realistic
one so there are young women who might have to face this coach
(metaphorically or specifically). If you change him, you have no
problem to explore. You have no scene. You have no dialogue. It's
magic. Talk with your group about magic and why it's antithetical
to the goals of this process. Stay away from magic and work from
the problem that's been presented. Replace the protagonist. After

spending some time on the protagonist you may decide to spend some time talking about the antagonist, exploring his motivations (two activities at the end of this section help in such cases). You may ask the group if there are other ways they can see the antagonist pressuring the protagonist in this situation. If there are and someone wants to try that, you could bring the original protagonist back up and play the scene anew. Then, you can facilitate it around the new pressure.

The Antagonist's Dilemma

Another challenge that arises around the antagonist is the fine line the actor playing the antagonist must walk between exerting pressure and being in the moment as a scene is replayed many times. The antagonist must pressure each replacing participant as hard (sometimes harder) as he did the original. Otherwise, it will be easy for the protagonists to "solve" the problem and others won't be activated to come up. The antagonist must be creative, strong, and unafraid to play tough with participants new to the scene. On the other hand, there does have to be a sense that the antagonist is listening and can be affected; otherwise, it seems hopeless and uninviting. Once again, improv skills and the feedback questions can help group members prepare for this and talk about how they did afterward.

> *"Magic" is when someone solves a problem by getting rid of the problem rather than dealing with it. Changing the circumstance, devaluing a relationship, or creating a kind supportive antagonist are forms of magic you will probably encounter. Ask the group if the new scene is magic; they'll know. Don't accept it.*

Prevent the Debate

Make certain that you keep audience comments addressed to you as you process the scenes. You want many interpretations so the group can learn from the multiple perspectives in the room, but you don't want participants debating each other over what they see or what is going on. Hear everyone out in moments of polarization and keep each person's focus on you. Your responsibility is to validate their individual contribution to the process with your attention, not your agreement. Likewise, you want to set up a dynamic where everyone's goal is to be heard, not to find unanimous agreement or support for their point of view. If you have a hot issue on the floor and you need to get a sense of where the group majority stands so you can move the process in a certain direction but you don't have time to hear every voice, use a yes/no question with a show of hands. "Raise your hand if you think the coach sexually harassed the girl in this scene." Show of hands. "How many people think he didn't?" Show of hands. "All right, let me hear from one person from each response, then we need to move on." It can be very helpful, quick, and inclusive.

Redirect the Exploration
If you have done some replacing and feel the energy is lagging, the situation is not holding the group's interest, or something simply isn't feeling right, requestion. Find other ways to ask the group to look at the scene.

Find other issues. For example, ask what the central issues are beyond the obvious one. Our scene is about sexual harassment. What else? Perhaps fear, power, control, authority, deceit, adult-youth conflict, trust (who will be believed), sexuality (Is there any part of her that is flattered, and what impact does that have?), and so forth. These words or ideas might open up a line of thought for someone (or for you) that leads to a whole other way of exploring options.

Play your ace in the hole. If you have been listening closely to all thoughts from the audience, you may have heard something early on that you could hold on to for the moment when things slow down. Early on in this scene, someone had mentioned that they felt the girl wanted the coach to acknowledge the inappropriateness of his actions. No replacement had yet dealt with that so I asked "What would be a satisfactory acknowledgment? What would the coach have to do or say? All right, someone try that." It took the scene in a new direction. It was my "ace in the hole." I saved it for later in the process. I often hold on to words that I can ask a group to look at more closely. Often, a group will say a protagonist wants support. After working a while, I may say "By the way, what is *support?*" It's usually ten different things. We then try to get some of those very specific things. Listen carefully and always keep thinking of other directions in which the exploration could go.

Change the circumstance. You could change the circumstance slightly or in a larger way. Present the idea and see if the group thinks it's realistic. In this scene, would the interaction take on new meaning if the coach was a friend of the girl's family? If the girl had abuse in her past? If the girl's home life was solid or troubled? If the girl was looking toward an athletic scholarship?

Gender flip. You can try the gender flip. This is a great tool for any scene. What if the coach were a woman also? What if they were both men? What if the situation was reversed and a woman was pressuring a man? There are tons of different dynamics, and chances to explore gender roles, stereotypes, and how all of this impacts choices and behavior in the scene. This raises another point as well. If you are facilitating a scene with a female protagonist, and a male audience member/participant wants to come up and replace (or vice versa), what do you do? Let them. But not at first. Start with a couple replacements of the same gender as the protagonist. Then if that person is interested in coming up, remind the group (the whole group, not just that person), that you expect everyone to respect the process. That means respecting the options that have been shared so far. That means not mocking them by coming up and being silly. Invite the person up, and if they are clowning, stop them, firmly but easily, and ask them to stay in the scene. If they continue to clown, stop them again and tell them they can sit down because other people have things they want to try. If they are doing something that seems like a stereotype but they seem to be in the scene, allow them to finish and then process with the group what they saw. Ask if they were able to see the option that was presented, or if they focused solely on the character. Push for honest feedback on stereotypes and the attitudes they may represent. You will most often get real replacements in these instances, but be prepared for anything.

Develop connecting scenes. You can take a scene anywhere you want to. If a group wants to see the protagonist try to tell her mother what has happened, you can do it. Have her mom not have time for her or not believe her, and you have a new activating scene. So long as you stay focused on the protagonist, stay away from magic, and don't create scenes that make everything OK because your group wants a happy resolution. Ask them to consistently face problems around the story and work to look for options. Some scenes might resolve as they play out. That's fine, but don't create a scene with the goal of tying up the loose ends and making everything OK. That's nullifying the struggles with which the characters are legitimately wrestling.

No Wrap-ups

A happy ending is not your goal. Your work on a scene ends when your time is up or when you feel you've played out the possibilities in the room at that moment; not when you have found the answer. It's not there. You do not want to finish by showing the group your idea of a good "solution." "Wrap-ups" basically discount all the exploration that has taken place and claim that a right way was waiting out there to be taught. That is the way some other curriculums use role plays: to give an answer and have individuals come up and practice. I don't buy that. Learning is the process that leads to practicing for real life. It is the process of actually finding our own methods to practice. You can wrap up work on a scene when the time is right by asking for overall impressions, discoveries, and reminding the group that choices are out there. You've examined some but certainly not all. Hopefully, everyone can use the experience to help them think out their own moments of decision.

A lot of the process rests on moments where you have to gauge where your group is at and where they want to go. Listen to them! There is no more important rule than that; when considering a couple of avenues for moving forward, present the options to the participants if you're unsure of which way to go. Be quick with accepting input. You don't want to bog the process down, but it is a wonderful way to share responsibility and to know if you're moving in the most productive direction.

Step 6: Further Exploration

Here are two other techniques for exploring the characters you're working with during the facilitation process.

Interviewing. After spending some time replacing the protagonist, this can be a great way to allow group members who haven't yet come up an opportunity to participate. Both actors stay in character and the audience questions them. It's like the interview in the Monologue activity you probably worked on earlier in the process with one significant difference. Here, the questions and responses should be brief and fast. You control the pace. People with questions put their hands up and you point at them and say "Go!" They have to be specific and direct their question at the appropriate character. You then point at the character and say "Go!" thus setting the rhythm and building the energy as you increase the tempo. They can ask anything, but they can't pass judgment and make comments. Look back at the Monologue activity for thoughts on the kinds of questions to push for.

You don't want to start with this because it can lessen a group's need to jump in and problem solve. It's a good activity to get them thinking fresh in the middle, while raising the energy level in the room, and it can be an interesting way to finish working on a scene. You can bring the original protagonist back up, or work with whoever is up at the moment if you think they can stay focused.

Fluid sculpting. This is the final phase of Machine, which was first introduced as a Warm-up, went further as a Bridge Activity, and was then used as a way to generate activating scenes in the Activating Material section. Here, it is a very powerful way to look at the inner voices that might be affecting either the protagonist, antagonist, or both as they make their choices in the scene you're facilitating. *Inner voices* are the thoughts, desires, and blocks that come from a myriad of people, times, and feelings in our lives; to quote Augusto Boal, "cops in our head" that stop us from taking care of ourselves and edge us towards things we don't really want to do.

For example, after working the scene about sexual harassment for a while, I might close by telling the group "I want us to take a moment and focus on the girl's inner life. I want us to see what might be going on inside." I would have the original protagonist stand in the middle of the room facing the rest of the group. Then I would tell all the participants that we are basically going to surround her with a machine of the thoughts and feelings you think are a part of her during this scene. "Any of you can come up, one at a time with a movement and an actual phrase, and add on to the machine. Create a living image of her inner life, a fluid sculpture."

The first person might come up, standing, hands moving back and forth to her face in shock, saying, "What do I do? What do I do?"

The next person might come up whispering in her ear, "Run. Run."

The next person might come up raising a fist and punching forward, saying, "I want to kill him! I want to kill him!"

The next person might come up serving a volleyball, saying, "You will not play junior varsity. You will not play junior varsity."

The next person might come up, sitting on the ground, looking up slowly, saying, "Does he find me attractive? Does he find me attractive?"

The next person might come up, shrugging, saying, "All right, so this is how it works here. All right, so this is how it works here."

You can get five to ten people up and then freeze the machine. Walk around and tap each person, having them do their sound and movement one time alone so everyone is seen and heard clearly. Then, you have some options:

- This can be your closing piece for the scene. You could do it for both characters or just one. You could talk about what was brought up or just let it rest as itself and go on. It's very powerful.
- You can have the rest of the group interview any of the individual voices and hear it out. The person who is the voice being interviewed maintains the movement and the attitude their phrase portrayed but is allowed to use other words. Their physical movement and their attitude become a filter for everything they say through the conversation. They are wearing the mask of the machine part they created. The person who said "Run. Run." is going to come from that point of view throughout the whole conversation. Their imagination will connect that point of view to the girl's life and help them answer any questions.
- You can match a part of the machine from the protagonist with a part of the machine from the antagonist, put them

together, and see how the scene changes when different parts of them are emphasized or deemphasized. You can even refacilitate from this point and allow group members to replace back into the scene.

There are many directions you could take fluid sculpting. The entire process can shift and bend to your goals and with your creativity.

Your Strength Is in Who You Are

Ultimately, who you are is where your success with this work lies. I have said that you must be energized. I have said that you must demand focus. I have said to make the experience fun. I would like to be clear that I know everyone has a different personality. I am not referring to a generic, cheerleading, exciting, theatre expert, super-educator type in every classroom. Some people initially get turned off of this work because they see it demanding a certain type of person, teacher, or community worker. *No.* Your strength is your own self and your own style. Young people respond to honesty, caring, and to someone as interested in listening as in talking. If you are willing to learn from youth, to challenge your creative self, to examine and possibly reconfigure your relationship with your group, to put aside "messages," and to trust in dialogue, you will find the experience of this process rewarding for those you work with and for yourself.

Stay focused on problem solving, exploring communication, and how the life experience each character (and every person) brings to an interaction affects their choices and their ability to follow through on those choices. And remember: It is work but it is also, most definitely, play.

Peer Education

Peer Education, Outreach, and Ongoing Group Work

Peer education means youths working with youths to raise awareness, instill activism, and problem solve around community issues through education. In the context of Hope Is Vital, education is dialogue; therefore, the training of youths to go out and conduct theatre-as-dialogue workshops is essentially the creation of a youth ensemble of artist/educators that can act as a resource in your community. The process gets broken down into three specific parts: (1) the training of the actual group, (2) the performance workshops the group leads in the community, and (3) the ongoing practice sessions that the group uses to stay dynamic and continue to grow. There are sample plans for workshops for all three of these parts in Appendix B. The work is what has been described in this book. But instead of developing an ongoing lab for exploration with one group, you are facilitating the development of a core group that will take that lab to others. The goals shifts a little. The group you train will experience the process as participants, but throughout the training, they must also be aware of the mechanics of that process. You must make time for specific moments to explore leadership dynamics, focus, and the nuts and bolts of activities at the same time that you are leading group members through the work itself. This way they will eventually be prepared to help lead the outreach sessions, ideally conducting the sessions themselves (with you present) after a certain point.

How do you navigate through various issues to maintain a Hope Is Vital group for the purpose of ongoing outreach work in your school and/or community? Keep in mind that although peer education has become popular and widespread lately, most peer education groups are doing presentational work. Even "teen theatre" work (usually youth-generated message plays) has very little in common with this program. Learn from their strategies of community involvement, fund-raising, and logistical structuring but know that the content and format of this work is very different. Stay grounded in dialogue.

The Adult and Youth Roles: Youth Driven, Adult Led

Your work with these techniques may have come about in a variety of ways. An existing group of peer educators may have decided to make interactive theatre their method of operation. A new student group may have formed around an issue, planning from the beginning to be based in interactive theatre techniques. Your school or community organization may have decided to form a youth group to start this program and you have been asked to organize and lead it. Or you may have started the ball rolling yourself, found youth, set up training, and begun. Any way the project is initiated, one thing remains true. One person (or a pair who will continue to work together) needs to lead the initial training. That one person (or persons) should be an adult and they should, ideally, be the person(s) who will continue with the group in a leadership capacity.

The process itself is a dialogue but it has an adult leader. "Youth driven" means that the youths in the group have active voices in the agenda, in the goals, in the scheduling, and in every aspect of the program. After the initial training, young people can lead some of the practice sessions and eventually move into facilitating performance workshops. Youths can take on the roles of scheduler (arrange times for practices and workshops and contact everyone), community liaison (contact potential sites for workshops and keep schools informed of peer educator schedules), and recruiter (keeping track of other youths interested in joining at the next turnover time).

It is the adult's responsibility to lead through a process *close* to consensus. Hear everyone out, but when decisions come along and the group has one weekly two-hour practice session, you won't want to spend the whole time on committee-style deliberations. If you have established a minicommunity of mutual respect and trust, you will be able to help move the process forward and sometimes simply make decisions yourself. Your two other main responsibilities are to consistently push the group to grow (through practice sessions and honest feedback after performance workshops) and to represent the group to the adult community. You are, no doubt, considered ultimately responsible in the eyes of your community for the program and its "content." It is important that you have honest conversations with your group about what issues you deal with in which settings, the age-appropriateness of certain scenes when you work with younger children, and the language used in improvisations. If you ever have concerns, you will make the final call. Take the time to talk about those concerns and community dynamics with your group, when and if they impact your outreach work.

Ground Rules

As I mentioned earlier, a conversation about ground rules at the beginning of a training process with peer educators is especially important because it sets the tone for how the peer educators will envision the performance workshops they will lead. It gives them a chance to discuss what they feel is important to make a space safe and it gives you a chance to stress the significance of their attention to these details when they work with others.

If not already mentioned by the youths, here are some of the rules I always bring up for discussion:

- **Confidentiality:** Everything said in the room stays in the room. We will be sharing stories, opinions, and looking silly together. We do that knowing it stays here.
- **Nonjudgment:** We agree to disagree. We listen to everyone and respect differences of all sorts. This is a safe place to be

heard (look at Values Clarification under Bridge Activities for more on this).

- **Respect:** We show respect in the way we talk to each other, listen to each other, take care of each other, and treat each other in every regard. This is very important from Day 1.
- **Openness:** Share what you can. Everyone gets as much out of this as they are willing to put in, not in terms of secrets or private stories, but of who you are and the degree to which you bring what is special in you to the group process.
- **Honesty:** When you choose to share, do so truthfully. Don't create stories to make an impression.
- **Right to pass:** You have the right to not participate in any activity if it makes you uncomfortable, and to do so without being interrogated as to why. Don't use this rule to step out just because you don't feel like playing; use your right to pass when you think the activity may be unsafe for you. You do always have that option. Take care of yourself.
- **Anonymity:** At some point in our process I'll give everyone a chance to write down a question or issue they would like the group to address. They may not want to "claim" the question so here is a chance to put it out there anonymously. All paper ends up in the middle, and we go through them one at a time.

Conducting Performance Workshops

The actual performance workshops that your group will conduct involve dynamics that are slightly different from ongoing group work. Some of those dynamics should be addressed here:

- In the beginning, you will want to facilitate performance workshops. After the group has conducted a few and had a chance to work on facilitation in practice sessions you can begin to allow youths to facilitate. This is dependent on there being interested youths who show skill as communicators and a willingness to truly listen and work on this very particular role. It is often helpful to identify one or two youths who will be the first youth facilitators, because one learns to facilitate by doing it. You will want to give them more time in practice sessions. If you want to move youth into this role early on, it makes more sense to have a couple of them at a higher level of competence than to have everyone at a lower level together.

- At performance workshops you may choose to have one facilitator for the whole session, or you may split up the duties and have different people lead different activities. In the case of the latter, the *connecting facilitator* is the person who speaks first, introduces the process, and gets it going. They return to introduce each new segment and activity leader. They also facilitate at least the first activating scene with the audience. The goal here is consistency for the audience, someone they develop a relationship with and with whom they grow comfortable. It brings a fluidity to the experience and increases audience participation.

- Fight for the time and space you know your group needs to succeed. You need a big room, not a cramped class with desks that don't move. You need more than 42 minutes. Push for 90 to 120 minutes. I know that's hard: Schedules; rules; you're considered pushy. It's OK. Be pushy. You are bringing a much needed resource to wherever you're going. Fight for the environment and the logistics that will make the experience successful for everyone involved.

- When you go out the audience usually has no idea what to expect. Many peer education groups shoot themselves in the foot by rushing through half-thought-out introductions and then saying "Let's play a game." Respect your audience. Take time in the beginning to ask them what they expect, to explain your goals, and to talk about the structure of what you will be doing. Here's one example:

> As peer educators, we've spent a lot of time talking about and struggling with issues we think young people deal with in our community. Rather than just tell you what we think or what you should think, we've come up with some ways to work on exploring these issues with you. We want to get a dialogue going in here today. That's our goal. We use theatre. This is a theatre workshop where we'll use theatre to ask some questions and you'll use theatre to help us look at some answers or options. For this

to happen we need your participation. We've got about half of what will happen in here today. You've got the other half. We're always learning about how this can work. We're really excited about it. We think you will be as well. We're going to start with some warm-up games to get us all moving around and playing together. It's important to us that we warm up together because of where we hope this session will lead. We have some scenes that we've created. These are realistic situations that we think can, and do, happen. We plan to share them with you and ask if they seem real. If they do, we want to know how you feel about the choices the characters made and what the characters wanted. If you want to see something different happen we're going to give you a chance to come up and show us other choices the characters could have made at key moments. You'll actually come up and do it. To work in this way we have to be willing to listen to each other, work together, and establish some respect and focus in this space. That's where we're going. First, let's play a game to help us warm up.

The communication of this must be *sincere, firm, energized, confident, unapologetic,* and *clear* in the voice of the speaker and in the body language of all group members in the room as they throw their energy behind the tone of this opening.

- From the moment your group walks in the door they are setting the tone for the workshop. They are being watched: every word they say, their posture, and their energy level all sends out signals. If they are unfocused, cliquish, or tired (before the session officially starts), you are already fighting an uphill battle. If they come in energized, introduce themselves to others in the room, and clearly want to be there, you are set up for success. They should spread out among the audience during the session, always establishing contact and trying to push others into involvement. They should participate in games, bridge activities, and activating scenes but only to make participation seem safe and fun. Their goal is to get audience members up and in, not to show off their skill in the work. They want to see as many participants try options in scenes as possible, so they shouldn't take up time with options of their own. If a session doesn't go well, *always,* ALWAYS have your group examine their own work and attitudes before blaming it on the audience. Appendix A is a postperformance workshop feedback sheet.

- Peer educators are going in to pose questions, not provide answers: to offer a safe place for honest dialogue and problem solving. Peer educators should not be bossy or think of themselves as "teachers in charge." They are educators and they are artists. They are there to facilitate with their peers. If being a peer educator becomes a power or status thing, have a conversation. Allow your goals and ground rules to act as reminders. Ask why people came to this group in the first place.

Practice Sessions

If you have an ongoing group doing outreach work in your school or community, these sessions are important. Here are some thoughts to consider.

Working sessions. They are about work, not socializing. Use the time you have together productively and let hang-out time occur before and after. They should be full-out, 100 percent work and play. People should be tired at the end. If the session is casual, the quality of your performance workshops will be casual.

Time. You want to meet, ideally, once a week for 2–3 hours. At the very least, every other week for 2 hours. You need time after the initial training to build on all the concepts and skills, and you also need to stay fresh in your scene work.

Leading activities. You should play warm-up games and bridge activities, giving different group members the opportunities to practice teaching and leading.

Improv. Improv, improv, improv. Remember, the imagination is a muscle. You must keep it exercised. Your work will get stronger and more interesting and your scenes will stay fresh. Play improv games that have nothing to do with issues. The energy will bleed into scenes you work on.

Develop activating scenes. Make it a goal to develop at least one new activating scene every practice session. That way you won't feel limited or stuck with old material. Also, group members can practice facilitating with these new scenes.

Performance workshop feedback. Give feedback from the last performance workshop if you've just had one. This is an important way to consistently get better.

Scheduling. Don't let scheduling be your downfall. Make schedules far in advance so people can plan their commitments around these practices. Have a conversation and determine the importance of each individual's commitment to the group practices. Should there be a contract regarding absences, excused or unexcused? Should someone who misses a practice session not participate in the next performance workshop? Should situations be dealt with as they arise? It is very hard for a group to grow when there is inconsistent participation in practice sessions.

Adding new members. After the initial training, at some point you may want or need to add new members. This is not to be handled lightly. You need to think about the best time and manner to bring them in. I recommend waiting six months to a year (when attrition has perhaps claimed some original group members) so that your initial group has a chance to solidify and get a sense of their work. Then have a new training. Perhaps not as long as the first one, but you need to spend a significant amount of time on group building. You are not just teaching the techniques to some new folks, you need to allow a new group dynamic to develop. Because the work is so collaborative and trust is so important, the experience almost needs to start over with each new configuration of people. Returning group members can certainly help mentor new ones, but be careful of a new versus old division that can lead to cliquishness. Design some sessions that demand everyone truly work together. Also, remember that getting youth with experience in theatre doesn't necessarily mean they have any experience with this type of theatre. They need to be willing to learn new approaches to performing and working with audiences.

Community Involvement

Because this work sometimes deals with sensitive issues and because it is based on a philosophy of education that is more revolutionary than standardized in this country, the program and the process can take on a curious mystique, at best, and at worst, an air of controversy or disapproval in a community. There might be confusion among adults as they grapple with the idea that you are using a dialogue program based on choices as opposed to teaching lessons. Your first step is to take the time to sit down with any and all interested (or specifically those disinterested) parties and talk about this work. Talk about dialogue as education, problem solving, affecting behavior through active learning, and exploring responsible and healthy decision making with groups.

The next and best thing you can do is to set up specific performance workshops with adults in the community. If possible, set up a session for group members' families. Get the parents advocating for you. Set up a session for school board members and administrators. Have an open performance workshop and invite local clergy, health workers, and law enforcement officials. Demystify the process and give everyone a chance to experience the power and the joy of this work. Here's the thing: these community involvement workshops must be *participatory* (which means you must limit the numbers and have a large enough space). Don't allow people to come as observers. The only way to learn about and appreciate this work is to engage in it. I'm not saying get them there and then force them to play. They can pass on anything at any time, but get them there as participants.

Also, don't open up your normal group performance workshops to observers. It changes the event and it will cause a lot of the youths in your audience to shut down. Have separate sessions with distinct purposes. Don't put your group in the position of auditioning the process or demonstrating it for stone-faced spectators. Invite and encourage curious community members (especially any causing trouble) to a session designed to expose them to and involve them in the process. In the session, they will actually have a chance to express themselves through scene work and to talk about the event as you close the session.

One Last Story

One of my favorite moments in a performance workshop involved a concerned community member who had been telling families to keep their kids away from this Hope Is Vital peer education group because he felt it was encouraging kids to have premarital sex. It was a small town, so word spread and the school became concerned. Up until then, the school had confidently supported the program. I was in town doing some retraining about a year after the program had started. The group and I decided to schedule a two-hour open session on a Friday night for youths and adults with a focus on youth, sex, and family communication. The idea was to try and get this man to come.

He did come, along with about 25 other community members and the existing peer education group of 14. There were a total of about forty people in the large basement space we were using. The group decided to include the activating scene about which the man had heard. In it a seventeen-year-old girl comes home to tell her dad that she is pregnant and gets thrown out of the house. The goal was to facilitate people up into the scene for the daughter and help her communicate with the father. She wanted support as she tried to figure out what to do. The workshop was going well. We talked about the process, warmed up, sculpted for a while, and then got to the scene about the father and daughter. So far, the man (let's call him Fred) had participated but was wary and detached. There was a certain tension in the room since most people knew Fred had been a vocal critic of the program lately and everyone was interested in how he was responding. So far, he wasn't. The scene played out. It was powerful and I began to facilitate, replacing the daughter two or three times. Then Fred stood up. He started talking loudly to the room in general, saying that we weren't dealing with the problem. He said the problem was that she had sex. The father's response was unimportant because she shouldn't have had sex in the first place.

I said "OK, that would also be a decision we could explore. We have a scene that looks at that choice, of having sex, but the youths we work with have said that this is also a realistic situation that could come up, and that it forces them to look at parent-child communication in a way that's helpful to them."

He said once again that it didn't matter what the daughter comes up and says. She made a mistake. She had sex. He began to lecture the room once again about abstaining, and the trouble the daughter was in.

I cut him off and said something to the effect of "I'm not going to let you lecture us. This workshop is a dialogue."

To which he responded, "See, you won't let me talk!"

Starting to get flustered, I said, "If you want to talk, talk in the scene. That's why we're here."

Before I knew what was happening, he had stormed up to the front and began yelling at his "daughter" (at this point, an audience participant) and telling her how she shouldn't have sex. He went on for almost a minute, starting very emotionally, getting calmer and more reasoned, then emotional again. When he finished, he stopped and looked at her.

There was a pause. She looked right at him. The room was silent. They were definitely in the scene.

She said, "Dad, I'm pregnant."

He looked at her and seemed to pull himself up to start lecturing at her again.

She took his hand and stopped him before he could start by saying, "Dad, I'm pregnant. I already had sex. It's too late for the speech."

He started to say, "How could you—"

She took his other hand, interrupted, and said, "Daddy, please. I don't know what to do. What should I do?"

He paused. He seemed to buckle a little and then she started to cry. After a moment, he opened up his arms and he held her.

She said, "Please don't make me go. Please."

Another pause, as she continued crying, and he just stood holding her.

After a few moments, he went back to his seat. He didn't want to talk about it. He didn't say anything else the rest of the session. We went on to the next activating scene. And Fred stayed through to the end.

I would not presume to say what, or if, Fred learned that night. It is true, however, that he didn't publicly oppose the group after that. I do know what I learned (or relearned) that night. In a moment given to me by a stranger I became more confident than ever in the mission and the means of this work.

Hope Is Vital does not declare right and wrong.
It does not seek single solutions.
It seeks discussion, trust, and
a step forward in each person's ability
to take care of themselves and
to look at their world with compassion.

Theatre allows us to converse with our souls, to passionately pursue and discover ways of living with ourselves and with others. We have no better way to work together, to learn about each other, to heal, and to grow.

Enjoy the process and the journey it takes you on. And remember, have fun.

Appendix A

Performance Workshop Feedback Sheet

Peer Educators: It is your responsibility to meet at least 15 minutes before each performance workshop to warm up and to stay at least 10 minutes after each performance workshop to have a brief feedback session. The adult leader of the group can facilitate the feedback session using this sheet as a guide, summarizing your thoughts and responses, writing them down here during the discussion, thinking about them before the next practice session, and then sharing their own feedback with the group at that time. This can help set the goals for the next practice session and make certain that you process the effectiveness of your work and needs for your own ongoing growth.

Group and Group Member Energy/Enthusiasm:

Group Teamwork and Focus:

Connecting Facilitator:

Activity Leading—Confidence and Clarity:

Scenes—Quality and Activation:

Facilitation of Scenes:

Appendix B

Sample Plans

Day 1 (3 hours)
Circle (Intros, Why everyone is here, Goals)
Cover the Space
Blind Handshakes
Blind (No Contact)
Storytelling
Ground rules talk
Trust Circle
Complete the Image
Two Revelations

Day 2 (3 hours)
Circle (to process Day 1)
Circle Dash
Find Your Mother Like a Little Penguin
Trust Pairs
Storytelling
Sculpting
Environment into a character variation

Day 3 (3 hours)
Circle (to process Day 2)
Machine as warm-up
Glass Cobra
Tour of a Place
Values Clarification
Zip Zap Zop
Circle Sculpt
Monologues

Day 4 (3 hours)
Circle (to process Day 3)
Cover the Space
Falling
Talk Improv
Activity/Urgency
Relationship Wheel
Russel's Soup (A/B)
Monologues (information sharing, if program plans to share information with youths)

Day 5 (3 hours)

Circle (to process Day 4)
Circle Dash
Circle Height
Russel's Soup (A/B), Line Improvs
Talk Activating Material
Machine as Bridge Activity
Group Storytelling/Sculpting
Groups create activating material
Examine activating material

Day 6 (6 hours)

Circle (to process Day 5)
Defender
Zip Zap Zop
Line Improvs
Monologues to activating material
Machine to activating material
Circle Sculpt to activating material
Anonymous questions
Donkey
Image Alive
Small groups to activating material
Work on facilitation

Day 7 (4 hours)

Circle (to process Day 6)
Donkey
Trust Circle
Exit
Entrance
Review activating material
Work on facilitation
Talk goals
Closure

Ongoing Peer Education Group Practice Sessions

Sample plans for first three practice sessions for peer-education group after initial training.

Session 1 (2 hours)
Circle (to talk about goals for practice)
Cover the Space (one peer educator leads)
Falling
Russel's Soup (A/B)
Work an activating scene or two from previous session
Work on group member facilitating
Circle Sculpt one new activating scene from an image
Reinforce information to be shared (if that's a part of the program)
Plan upcoming performance workshop

Session 2 (2 hours) (some time after 1st performance workshop)
Circle (for feedback from performance workshop)
Machine
Zip Zap Zop
Line Improvs
Small groups create new activating scenes
Environment (quick round) with characters from activating scenes
Work Facilitating and Fluid Sculpting

Session 3 (2 hours)
Circle (to process last practice and where people are at)
Circle Dash
Blind (No Contact) (sound variation)
Complete the Image
Image Alive
Machine to an activating scene
Plan next performance workshop

> ## Classroom Work
> *Sample plan for a class focusing on an issue for ten 45-minute
> sessions (10–40 youths, 20–30 ideal)*

Session 1
Circle, Intros, Goals
Cover the Space
Blind Handshakes
Blind (No Contact)
Storytelling
Ground rules

Session 2
Circle (to process Session 1
   briefly)
Refresh ground rules
Circle Dash
Find Your Mother Like a Little
   Penguin
Complete the Image

Session 3
Circle (to process Session 2)
Tilt
Trust Circle
Trust Falls
Storytelling around issue
   (subtly)

Session 4
Circle (to process Session 3)
Machine as warm-up
Sculpting

Session 5
Circle (to process Session 4)
Cover the Space
Zip Zap Zop
Two Revelations
Talk Improv

Session 6
Circle (to process Session 5)
Environment
Activity/Urgency
Values Clarification

Session 7
Circle (to process Session 6)
Donkey
Relationship Wheel
Russel's Soup (A/B)
Line Improvs

Session 8
Circle (to process Session 7)
Line Improvs
Talk activating material
Circle Sculpt to create activating
   material
Facilitation

Session 9
Circle (to process Session 8)
Machine
Machine as bridge to activating
   material
Facilitation

Session 10
Circle Dash
Activating material work
Facilitation
Process issues, problem solving
   techniques, and strategies

One-Shot Workshops
*Sample plan for a 3-hour, one-shot session with a group
around an issue (10–60 people, 25–40 ideal)*

Circle, Intros, Expectations, Goals
Cover the Space
Blind Handshakes
Blind (No Contact)
Storytelling
Complete the Image
Sculpting

Two Revelations
Circle Sculpt
Take an image and create an
    activating scene
Facilitation
Process the session

---

*Sample plan for a 90-minute to 2-hour session that a 12-person
peer education group might lead with 25 high school students*

Circle (if possible), Intros, Goals
Circle Dash
Blind Handshakes
Small Group Sculpting
Circle Sculpt

Present group-created activating
    scenes (1 or 2) and facilitate
    them
Share information (if that is part of
the program)
Closure

Appendix C

Resources: Books

These are books that will be helpful in finding theatre activities, exploring the concepts further, and getting a sense of how others use theatre in education and community work.

The first one to get:
AUGUSTO BOAL. 1992. *Games for Actors and Non-Actors*. Routledge.
Although Hope Is Vital is not straight Boal work, his insights and activities are invaluable to anyone doing theatre and community dialogue work.

Others to get as quickly as you can:
ROBERT ALEXANDER. *Improvisational Theatre for the Classroom: A Curriculum Guide for Training Regular and Special Education Teachers in the Art of Improvisational Theatre.*
Call Living Stage at (202) 234-5782, and they will sell and ship you a copy of this training booklet.
AUGUSTO BOAL. 1995. *The Rainbow of Desire*. Routledge.
VIOLA SPOLIN. 1986. *Theatre Games for the Classroom*. Northwestern University Press.
JAN COHEN-CRUZ AND MADY SCHUTZMAN, EDS. 1993. *Playing Boal: Theatre, Therapy, Activism*. Routledge.
DOROTHY HEATHCOTE AND GAVIN BOLTON. 1995. *Drama for Learning: Dorothy Heathcote's Mantle of the Expert Approach to Education*. Heinemann.
ANTHONY JACKSON, ED. 1993. *Learning through Theatre: New Perspectives on Theatre in Education*. Routledge.
EVONNE HEDGEPETH AND JOAN HELMICH. 1996. *Teaching about Sexuality and HIV*. New York University Press.
A wonderful overview of strategies, learning styles, and activities around these issues that also persuasively makes the case for the dialogue-based approach that Hope Is Vital utilizes.

Others that are great to have:

PAOLO FREIRE. 1993. *Pedagogy of the Oppressed.* Continuum Publishing.

AUGUSTO BOAL. 1985. *Theatre of the Oppressed.* Theatre Communications Group.

VIOLA SPOLIN. 1983. *Improvisation for the Theatre.* Northwestern University Press.

GERALD CHAPMAN. 1990. *Teaching Young Playwrights.* Heinemann.

JOSEPH CHAIKIN. 1991. *The Presence of the Actor.* Theatre Communications Group.

NIGEL DODD AND WINIFRED HICKSON, EDS. 1971. *Drama and Theatre in Education.* Heinemann.

CLIVE BARKER. 1988. *Theatre Games.* Methuen.

WILLIAM AYERS AND PATRICIA FORD, EDS. 1996. *City Kids, City Teachers: Reports from the Front Row.* The New Press.

ZAKES MDA. 1993. *When People Play People: Development Communication through Theatre.* Zed Books.

PAOLO FREIRE. 1996. *Letters to Cristina.* Routledge.

IRA SHOR. 1996. *When Students Have Power: Negotiating Authority in a Critical Pedagogy.* University of Chicago Press.

VIVIAN GUSSIN PALEY. 1992. *You Can't Say You Can't Play.* Harvard University Press.

LEON DASH. 1990. *When Children Want Children: An Inside Look at the Crisis of Teenage Parenthood.* Penguin Books.

MARY PIPHER. 1995. *Reviving Ophelia: Saving the Selves of Adolescent Girls.* Ballantine Books.

Appendix D

Resources: Contacts

To find out about the annual Pedagogy of the Oppressed conference and corresponding Theatre of the Oppressed workshops conducted by Augusto Boal in Omaha, NE, contact:

Omaha's Public Theatre In Our Neighborhoods (OPTION)
(Center for Theatre of the Oppressed - Omaha)
Doug Paterson
(402) 554-2422
E-mail:
paterson@fa-cpacs.unomaha.edu

In the Seattle area, to take advanced classes utilizing some of the techniques in this work, contact:

Seattle Public Theatre
Mark Weinblatt
(206) 328-4848

In Washington, DC, to participate in Living Stage improvisational workshops for educators and community workers, contact:

Living Stage
(202) 234-5782

To talk to someone about the experience of setting up a university campuswide program utilizing this work, contact:

Carol Day
Georgetown University
in Washington, DC
(202) 687-8942

To talk to someone about the experience of using this work as the basis of a communitywide outreach program, contact:

Elizabeth Allbrecht
Planned Parenthood
in Portland, OR
(503) 775-3918
or
Irene Addlestone
Children's National Medical Center
in Washington, DC
(202) 884-5449

To talk to someone about the experience of using this work as the basis for an ongoing peer education group in a high school, contact:

Jon Aaron
McDonough School
in Baltimore, MD
(410) 363-0600

*To talk to someone about the
experience of using this work as
the basis for conducting teacher
trainings in a community, contact:*

Tracy Wiseman
Douglas County Health
Department
(402) 444-7226
E-mail:
twiseman@co.douglas.ne.us

*To find out more about Hope Is
Vital trainings, residencies,
workshops, and conference sessions,
contact:*

Michael Rohd
Founder and Director
(541) 341-0747
(410) 363-6282
E-mail: Mrohd@aol.com